EMOTIONS
AND THE
ENNEAGRAM

Other books by Margaret Frings Keyes:

The Enneagram Cats of Muir Beach
Molysdatur Publications, Muir Beach, California 1990
Inward Journey: Art as Therapy
Open Court Publishing Company, La Salle, Illinois
(revised edition 1983)

EMOTIONS
AND THE
ENNEAGRAM
Working Through Your
Shadow Life Script

Margaret Frings Keyes

Molysdatur Publications, Muir Beach, California
1990

The following publishers have generously given permission to use quotations from copyrighted works: Excerpts from "Burnt Norton" and "East Coker" in *Four Quartets*, copyright 1943 by T.S. Eliot and renewed by Esme Valerie Eliot, reprinted by permission of Harcourt Brace Jovanovich, Inc. and Faber & Faber Ltd. "In a Dark Time", copyright © 1960 by Beatrice Roethke, Administrix of the Estate of Theodore Roethke. From *The Collected Poems of Theodore Roethke* by Theodore Roethke. Used by permission of Doubleday, a division of Bantam, Doubleday, Dell Publishing Group, Inc. and Faber & Faber Ltd.

Library of Congress Cataloging-in-Publication Data
I.   Keyes, Margaret Frings
II. Title   1. Emotions   2. Enneagram   3. Psychoanalysis
4. Individuation   5. Peace-making   6. Conflict-resolution
techniques   7. Transactional Analysis   8. Archetypal Psychology.
Library of Congress Card No.: 88-62552

ISBN 1-882042-04-2

Originally published as *Out of the Shadows: Uses of Depression, Anxiety, and Anger in the Enneagram* by Molysdatur Publications, Muir Beach, California 1988.

The opinions expressed in this book are those of the author. They are not derived from, and do not represent, the teachings of any institution or school. We build on each other's insights, however, and sources are credited whenever possible.

Molysdatur books are distributed by Publishers Services, P.O. Box 2510, Novato, CA 94947.

Design by Paula Morrison
Cover photo and illustrations by Stanton Nelson
Author's photo by Michelle Vignes
Typesetting by ExecuStaff, Los Gatos, California
Printing by Consolidated Printers, Berkeley, California

For Kathleen, Peter and Lucia
who integrate the inner and outer world
with grace and courage.

Table of Contents

Part II: "That You Become the Person Only You Can Be"

Diagrams and Charts

Acknowledgements

In the early 1970s, the Jesuit priest Bob Ochs introduced me to the Enneagram. This system for understanding personality types seemed to offer a special perspective on the Shadow Archetype, the difficult, obsessive aspects of the person, first described by Carl G. Jung. It dealt with the three forms of pain people bring to therapy—depression, anxiety and anger. It also connected an unusual number of behaviors, attitudes and values to each of these feelings. These connected attributes correspond to Jung's concept of unconscious complexes.[1]

In the years that followed, Jane Lipman of Taos, New Mexico, Suzanne Baldwin of Denver, Colorado and Helen Palmer of Berkeley, California shared their insights with me. Helen Palmer, who founded the Center for the Investigation and Training of Intuition, generously allowed me the use of the CITI videotapes while I was writing this book. In these tapes, she used students to depict each Enneagram point and, through questioning, drew out their essential characteristics and preoccupations.

Helen's clear and precise thought contributed to the core of my program descriptions. Her imprint is evident in all descriptions of the essential Point characteristics and preoccupations. My book, however, emphasizes the Enneagram as an early life choice for dealing with difficult emotions. It reframes the feelings in terms of Shadow issues, to open choice again in the individual's inner life and outer world.

Donald T. Brown, M.D.'s seminars linking General Systems Theory to Group Process, and Hector Sabelli, M.D.'s analysis of the vectors of conflict have been major influences on my thought. Louis Bartolucci, M.D. has pointed my attention to relevant research on the human brain, and limited my generalizations. He has also been my unfailing consultant in every computer problem I have faced in producing this material.

I am grateful to Doris Arrington and other faculty members of Notre Dame College, Belmont, California, who appointed me to the

Catherine Julie Cunningham Chair during the fall of 1984. My study of the Collective Shadow Archetype took place then. Several people helped me to understand how emotions work: my long-ago mentors Eric Berne, Fritz Perls and Jo Wheelwright; also my friends in psychodrama, Mary Gerber, Dorothy Satten and particularly John Argue, a trainer of actors and gestaltists. John, who has closely observed and identified the physical body components of strong feeling-states, taught me to see with more than my eyes. I am grateful to John Enright for identifying the healing function of humor and aggression in the Synanon Game. Scott O'Keefe and John Lavine were invaluable in shaping the material for presentation. Bill Chapin, Linda Remy, James Folliard and Stan Nelson critiqued my writing at crucial points. My fellow Muir Beach writers Larry Stump, Leba Wine and Judith Yamamoto helped immeasureably in the initial reading of the manuscript, and Marie Hayward in the final preparation.

Addendum: An earlier version of this book, published as OUT OF THE SHADOWS: Uses of Depression, Anxiety and Anger in the Enneagram, was distributed for critical comment and proofreading. Sold at production cost, mostly to professional colleagues, the books produced significant reader response. The current edition has benefited and been substantially revised. This edition continues the author's primary goal to provide further insight into Enneagram concepts of personality in the light of Jungian psychology.

Readers interested in the occult and esoteric origins of the Enneagram or the Enneagon theory of Oscar Ichazo are referred to the Arica Institute, Inc., 150 Fifth Avenue, #912, New York, NY 10011. The author's view of the Enneagram in the light of Jungian psychology would probably be considered a distortion by Aricans rather than an extension of Enneagon theory.

Margaret Frings Keyes
San Francisco, California   February 1990

Preface

For centuries we have been taking notes on ourselves and each other. We have noticed how things hang together, and we have considered everything about human behavior. Many of our ancestors coded their earliest, astute observations in stories, supposedly about the gods.

Today we see these myths as patterns describing the human condition. For example, the stories of Hera and Zeus investigate jealousy in marriage between a strong-willed woman and her philandering husband. Today's novelists such as John Updike and Marge Piercy continue to investigate the same questions in contemporary society.

The pull of opposing emotional choices is the stuff of human drama. We watch, absorbed, as a tragic event unfolds, whether it's a governmental scandal or a movie episode. Conflict captures our attention. In normal life, for the most part, we cooperate with one another. Inevitably, however, disputes occur and anger or fear irrupts, each provoking an action in response—to fight or to flee. When we win, we feel elated; when we escape we feel relieved; but if we have to submit, we feel depressed.

Major Behavior Programs

Distinct body responses, including blood chemistry changes, accompany our emotional changes. As we learn more about the structures of the human brain, how we take in and screen information, we realize that the patterns we have been observing might be viewed as mind programs.

Each of us apparently creates a unique set of responses to meet our survival, sexual and social needs. These programs operate below consciousness. They give precise instructions regarding what signals to heed, what information to screen, what emotions to release, and even what choices to see. Implicitly some data are not seen and some choices are avoided, or screened out.

We develop our primary programs from childhood experiences. Particular feeling responses, repeated and reinforced, become a child's program. With reasonable stress the child develops appropriate strength, and the program becomes a flexible style of personality. On the other hand, depending on the severity of the threats and how early in life the child had to face them, defensive programming can become rigid. Various degrees of disability in carrying out life's tasks then result. The child doesn't fully develop. The neurotic doesn't gain a full sense of how to manage a job or be a friend. The psychotic constructs an inner picture of the world immensely different from the one in which the rest of us function.

Psychological theories and some religious disciplines attempt to describe these programs, although they may not think of them as such. They use other terms and emphasize different parts.

This book explores the varying ways emotions interact with thoughts and action in nine body/mind programs. It uses behavioral descriptions developed from the Enneagram. (Enneagram, a Greek word, means "nine points" and refers to a classification of nine personality types.) A shift toward a less defended, more inclusive reality becomes possible through conscious work. This work fits closely with what we know of the essential stages identified in most spiritual traditions.

The Enneagram does not contradict but extends theories of human behavior as different as behaviorism and Jungian analysis. For example, nine distinctly different versions of Jung's notion of the Shadow archetype can be inferred from it. Furthermore, as in behaviorism, we can identify specific behavior we reject and avoid—and the price we pay for change in any given program. The Enneagram suggests that wrestling with a distorted emotional cluster develops a unique strength; once we have overcome the flaw, we transform it into a particular asset.

The Enneagram's difficulty is that it is the centerpiece of an esoteric tradition with a freightload of distractions, accumulated meanings, and cumbersome speculations. In unpacking that freight, this book explores only the emotional content involved. It does not intend to represent the full teachings of the Enneagram. The emotional patterns, however, offer unique insights which deal with the dark and unacceptable forces and threats we feel in our personal lives and in the outer world. We find these Shadow patterns of the individual mind reflected in patterns of interaction among small and large social groups, including nations.

The Enneagram

The Enneagram is said to have originated in Afghanistan almost 2000 years ago and to have been taught as part of a secret oral tradition among Sufis in the following centuries.

In Provence around 1250 there seems to have been some interconnection between the Enneagram and the Sefirot figure of the Kabbala, an esoteric interpretation of Hebrew Scriptures. Mathematical constructs connect the Enneagram with the Kabbala, and suggest the possibility that the nine personality types evolve potentially into nine aspects of the One God.[1]

George Ivanovich Gurdjieff, born in the Caucasus during the 1870s, was a student of Sufi, Indian, Tibetan and Christian mystical traditions. He successfully taught mysticism in the West in the first half of this century. Among others, the author Doris Lessing and the architect Frank Lloyd Wright were heavily influenced by his thought.

One of Gurdjieff's teaching tools was the Enneagram, which he described as perpetual motion. He compared it metaphorically to the philosophers' stone (which turns lead into gold) sought by the early alchemists.[2] Jung, depicting alchemical symbolism as the language of the psyche, would later use the philosopher's stone in his studies to represent the unified Self, the goal sought by all spiritual and psychological disciplines.

Whatever else it may be, the Enneagram connects and unifies information ranging from music to psychology. Today it has entered the language of psychology following its introduction into the United States by Oscar Ichazo.[3]

Claudio Naranjo, a Chilean-born psychiatrist now living in Berkeley, California, matched the pathological form of each Enneagram point to the *DSM III* (the *Diagnostic and Statistical Manual of Mental Disorders, Third Edition*), the current classification system for mental disorders.[4] That is to say, each of the nine behavioral programs has a range of intensity. The more encased a person's behavior is in the program, the closer he or she is to psychotic behavior, which we can describe in terms of the *DSM III*. When his identification is lighter, he carries his program as a personality style with specific strengths. The strengths develop as he wrestles with the point's Shadow issues and preoccupations.

Helen Palmer has used the Enneagram as a tool to identify and develop each point's latent intuitional skills. The psychologist Charles Tart, the Jesuit Bob Ochs and many other students of the Enneagram have developed their own teaching emphasis.

Clearing Programs and Waking to a Wider Reality

What's the use of such knowledge? When we view our brain's system of filters, screens and triggering processes in the light of the program descriptions, we can broaden our perspective to include more information. Psychedelic drugs used to fascinate users because they overwhelmed the filters and brought in sensory data usually shunted off as irrelevant to everyday concerns. However, the drug experience did not allow integration; in contrast, when we understand what our mind programs tend to screen out, we restore our choice to include these perceptions.

It is not only intellectual work; it requires a different use of our negative feelings—depression, anxiety and anger. We have to deal with the problems and the possibilities that inclusion presents. But knowing ourselves more deeply connects us with a new sense of joy, appreciation and wonder. We grasp the purpose of our existence: to know, love and serve Life.

Studying the programs allows us to understand our own beginnings and appreciate what children need to develop their capacities. Societal influences both help and hinder healthy emotional functioning. We develop hunches about how to heal and educate those who have been severely wounded; these hunches allow us to view the wounded differently, as closer kin.

Finally, many of us want to connect with a wider and deeper reality in ourselves and the outer world. We are curious about what mystics claim lies outside the boundaries of ordinary consciousness. Creativity and spontaneity attract us, and we want these attributes as much as possible.

Some beginning exercises, information about different paths and the consequences of following them are in a section after the program descriptions. The second half of the book moves our attention to the outer world. It identifies a strategy to understand how we define an enemy, how we can identify bonds of connection between "us" and "them," and how to move toward a resolution of our differences which will allow us to survive. We live in a set of patterns, but in understanding those patterns we become free to choose.

The final segment of the book returns to our individual Enneagram programs and presents a process which allows us to identify our specific points of access and influence in the wider world community. Because each of us is deeply connected with everyone and everything else, our choices matter.

Part I:

"We Live Side by Side in Different Worlds"

Introduction:

"To Know What We Feel and to Feel What We Know"

As children, bit by bit, we build a picture of the people around us and what we have to deal with in our lives. We don't quite see the same world that our family sees. Our senses, our language, our family, our socially agreed-upon fictions, and mostly our experiences and decisions from childhood, condition us to select certain realities and suppress the rest. We put these ideas together in a way that makes sense to us, a way that tells us how to survive and meet our needs. When we use this model to make decisions, we create a strategy or program for living.

Most of us have programs that work well. Others have models in which perceptions are blocked and thought is badly distorted by fear, anger or depression.

To understand the linkage between thought and feeling, imagine that you are driving home from work. Just before you left the office, your boss returned a project you thought you had completed, saying that you had overlooked something and would have to redo the whole thing. Your thoughts still preoccupy you as you start into an intersection. The yellow light turns red and you have to jam on your brakes to avert a collision with a speeding car entering from a side street.

Depending on how you've programmed your brain, you might now find yourself—

      opening your car to get into the street, feeling outraged and focused on the other driver's violations, ready to take him on in combat, verbally or physically.

      sitting in the car, ashen-faced, weak-muscled, feeling terrified that you have been so close to death.

sitting in the car, focused on your failure to stay alert, blaming yourself for your risk taking with the yellow light, and feeling depressed with this further evidence of your inability to cope with your life.

shaken but aware that both drivers contributed to the near accident and resolving to put the office matters on hold until the next day.

What is going on inside to account for these differences?

In our example, you tied up a good amount of your energy recycling work issues. You were driving on "automatic pilot," which is usually quite sufficient for a trip home. Something happened, however. The low-level automatic scanning changed to high alert with the changing visual perception (red light/car approaching from side street).

Your brain generated emotions. It compared incoming stimuli from inside and outside the body with its programmed instructions based on your earlier experiences. Next it signaled for an emotional and muscular response, when the incoming stimuli (red light/car coming fast) did not fit the expected patterns. Impulses then triggered the release of hormones which caused your feelings of anger, fear or anxiety. This response increased adrenalin and blood sugar, sped up your heart rate, and did other things which prepared your body to fight, flee, or submit to the new data the brain assumed to be dangerous.

Emotions help us to survive. They push us to do what we associate with safety, pleasure and well-being. You didn't pause to think and decide. Your foot jammed on the brake and you braced yourself.

While this is happening in one part of the brain, another part apparently acts in an opposite way; it helps to cool us down and to release our emotional tension. When we focus conscious thought on finding the most appropriate response, we experience a physical calming. Adrenalin reduces and the heart quiets. In our example, this happened when you decided to put the office matters on hold.

Personality Programs for Behavior

Although we do not know precisely how neurotransmitters work, each child's brain seems to create a set of programs having to do with self-preservation, sexuality and social needs. These programs

4

influence that child's emotions, perceived choices and behavior, even when there is no emergency.

According to the gestalt theory of perception, whatever we fear, desire, expect or demand occupies a larger share of our attention than neutral stimuli. When we are hungry, we notice food and places to eat more than when we are well fed. When we are angry, we are more sensitive to provocations. Our brain filters incoming sensory information and interacts with our programming to reinforce the world model already created. It sends on only information of interest to our chosen program.

In sudden stress, one characteristic response overrides all others; this feeling is a variant of anger, fear or helpless depression.

These feelings are not difficult to notice, only difficult to anticipate. We usually become aware of fear, jealousy, anger, sadness or emotional numbing only after an ego-state program has been triggered and we are already responding automatically in words and interactions with other people. When we become aware of our habitual feeling responses, we also may notice recurring thoughts. These help to identify how our mind functions. Habitual feelings and thoughts block other, possibly more appropriate, responses. To stop a program, it is necessary to give ourselves repeated and firm instructions to eliminate the old filters and replace them with a more inclusive reality base. Various spiritual and psychological disciplines have been developed to do this.

Each of the nine life strategies of the Enneagram which follow has an addictive central preoccupation. In each strategy, a Shadow distortion or flaw has to be overcome to acquire a specific strength (in older terminology, a "virtue"). What was rejected has to be faced. The stress-response feelings of depression, anxiety and anger have to be valued as tools and used differently. As this happens, one becomes an individual, integrated human being.

Now, for a description of the Programs.

Depression, Anxiety and Anger in Enneagram Behavior: The Perpetual Motion of the Enneagram

Each point connects to two other points on the circle. When life conditions change, a person first responds by going deeper into *his own point's* defenses. As the stress increases, he moves with the arrow

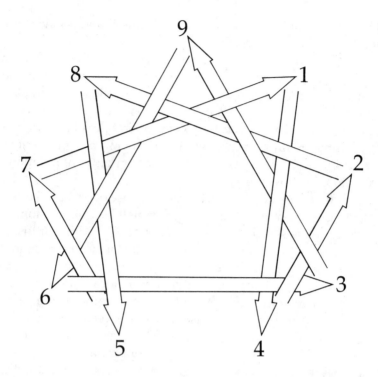

to behavior more characteristic of *the following point*. In times of low stress, his behavior is more expansive, and can take on the characteristics of *the preceding point*.

The arrows, moving ONE—FOUR—TWO—EIGHT—FIVE—SEVEN—ONE on the outer star, follow a mathematical sequence connected to the Enneagram's esoteric origin.[2]

The inner triangle connects points THREE—SIX—NINE; each of these three Programs has two associated Programs dealing differently with the core feeling (depression, anxiety or anger).

Enneagram Emotions in Response to Danger

This diagram represents a clinical view of emotion as our means for mobilizing and releasing energy. *All* feelings are present in each of us, but we differ in our readiness to recognize particular feelings. The defensive mode prevents movement from our Program and covers other, more appropriate feelings. For example, Programs EIGHT, NINE and ONE use *anger* as the chosen response to stress. Sometimes anger is focused appropriately, not as a fixed response;

but when we habitually respond to stress with overt anger (EIGHT), passive aggression (NINE) or resentment (ONE), this indicates an Enneagram distortion.

Similarly, *fear* is an appropriate response to real danger and is present (directly or indirectly) in all Programs, but we vary in our ability to accurately sense and respond to threat. People in Programs FIVE, SIX and SEVEN are highly sensitive to all forms of danger. However, when withdrawal (FIVE), phobic or counter-phobic behavior (SIX) or distraction (SEVEN) is the inappropriate or disproportionate response to most stress, an Enneagram distortion exists.

Programs TWO, THREE and FOUR, in contrast, characteristically repress unguarded feeling responses of fear or anger. Submission to a dominant-person or performance Program allows us to avoid fighting or fleeing. Instead, we respond to the other person's feelings (TWO), the other's approval (THREE), or a fantasy or other symbolic displacement of true feelings (FOUR). There is a peculiar pride or vanity in meeting external standards of peformance in a way that establishes us as superior. An underlying *depression*, evidence of feelings being shut down, becomes evident only when stress is overwhelming.

The Enneagram Programs

Structure of the Descriptions

Each Program describes a focal parent-child issue. Through actions and words, parents give their children both their conscious and subconscious understanding of life's opportunities and dangers. The descriptions simplify these into injunctive messages to show the type of instruction the child receives.

Over time, the strategy which the child employs for dealing with his or her plight results in an Enneagram Program with a stress response of depression, anxiety or anger. A paragraph in italic type, similar to this one, identifies it.

The Programs are given in groups of three, corresponding to the stress responses. In the stories and examples of Program functioning, real-life names and the circumstantial details have been changed to protect confidentiality. A chart precedes each Program description, and it notes major characteristics of the Program as follows:

Self-Description: A phrase which the person might use to describe his or her own behavior. For example, ONE's "I'm hard working."

Shadow: The negative issue or unacceptable attribute which the person must wrestle with to achieve personal integration.

The personal Shadow takes a different form in each Enneagram Program. As the part of us that resists our conscious wish to be perfect, to have no faults, venal feelings or shifty attitudes, the Shadow embarrasses us. Even when we are aware of our Shadow issue, e.g., FOUR's envy, it is a continuing force from our unconscious which takes many shapes.

Rejected Element Needed for Transformation: An overlooked and avoided feeling or experience needed to complete one's personal integration. For example, when EIGHT owns (acknowledges) personal weakness, the possibility of healing comes.

Addiction: A compulsion the person treats as a basic need. For instance, ONE's perfectionism.

Strength Needed: The particular attribute which the person gains from conscious work with the Program's problems and issues. An example of this is FIVE'S detachment.

Defense Mechanism: The characteristic psychological defense the person uses in times of stress (one of the forms of fight, flight or submission), such as SIX's projection.

Psychological Disturbance: The form of mental illness associated with extreme distress. For example, SIX's paranoia.

Preoccupations: General concerns of the strategy together with the dominant emphasis of each sub-type.

Focus: A further division occurs within each Enneagram. One of three drives tends to dominate the person's instinctual life. Each person's passionate energy is directed toward personal survival concerns, intimacy with one other person, or toward the needs of the group—toward one person, the couple, or the community. The latter can be political or altruistic.

A *personal* focus characterizes those persons whose primary passion is survival. People whose sexual drive is the strongest instinct, or whose primary concern is relationship to one other person, have a *couple* focus. Those whose passions are primarily political or related to group concerns have a *community* focus.

Life Task: The work here is to become a fully realized individual. Each description includes a diagram which shows the two alternative Programs associated with each strategy.

Classification starts with naming. The usual designation of Enneagram points is by number or by ego-state distortion as originated by Oscar Ichazo. For our purposes, the behavior descriptions which follow are seen as Programs: the outer evidence of a systematic way we take in information about the outer world, organize our feelings and limit our choices of possible action.

For instance, number ONE is therefore designated the *Program of Perfection With Resentment*. This emphasizes not only the feeling of resentment, which threads through the thoughts of the individual, but also the Program's preoccupation with perfection. The Program names contain tension. The first descriptive word, in a sense, is the justification for the behavior chosen, such as perfection or helpfulness; this quality takes on an addictive or compulsive aspect. The second descriptive word, the negative companion of the justification, holds a potent energy for change. Resentment, manipulation or whatever must be transformed before it can be used.

Descriptions are in the third person. Because each Enneagram describes both genders and use of the formula "he or she" is awkward, I have used the plural "they" when feasible and alternated use of the singular form. When either "he" or "she" is used, both are intended.

It always seems easier to classify other people than to identify and accept our own Shadow issues. "Hey, I'm not stingy!" "What do you mean, vengeful?" Nonetheless, as you read the Enneagram programs you will find several points that feel familiar, and you'll remember dealing with similar themes at different times in your life. You might read the descriptions through, then return to the one which seems most familiar to you and shift the "they", "she," or "he" form to "I," to check its personal fit.

Groups often act in ways that resemble Enneagram Programs. Some systematically influence the formation of such mindsets within people. Each Program description includes one or more of these groups to give a broader picture of the patterns.

Chapter One:

The Programs of Submission/Depression

The Program of Helpfulness with Manipulation
The Program of Achievement with Emphasis on Image
The Program of Excellence with Moody Nostalgia

Photo by Stanton Nelson

A dog rolls over and exposes its neck. The top dog growls, but does not attack further. Dominance, "who's in charge," has been established.

It seems ludicrous to compare a highly successful corporate executive to the underdog. Perhaps it's easier to define the charming, manipulative woman who glories in her powerful husband that way, but surely not the man. Take another example, the creative, well-known entertainer who struggles with bouts of depression—what have these behaviors to do with submission?

Submission occurs whenever one puts down, consciously (suppression) or unconsciously (repression), a vital instinct or energy in the interest of safety or survival. The corporate executive who has become the successful competitor by suppressing aspects of himself which do not fit the "winner image" has submitted to outer cultural norms. The woman who has repressed her own needs and now identifies with her husband's power has submitted to a cultural norm that women should be helpful rather than powerful. The entertainer who works to gain the approval of his audience may be *depressed*, avoiding a deeper sadness which he needs to experience and finish.

A style and pattern of submission can be set in childhood when the child accepts the adult worldview, replacing his or her sense of what is so. Fulfilling the expectations of others provides approval which substitutes for other desires. But depression lurks a hair's breadth away. Paradoxically, it often offers the first step out of a life of unconscious, addictive habits and into one's personal reality.

Enneagram programs TWO, THREE and FOUR explore three major variations in perceived threats, submissive patterns and steps necessary for release.

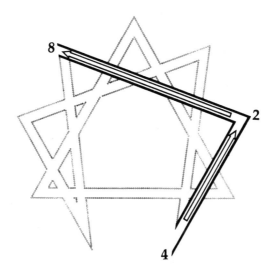

Point Two: The Program of Helpfulness With Manipulation

Self-Definition: "I'm helpful."

Shadow Issue: Parasitic pride

Rejected Element: One's own needs

Addiction: Service/manipulation

Strength Needed: Appropriate self-value (Humility)

Defense Mechanism: Repression

Psychological Disturbance: Hysteria/dependent personality

Preoccupations Include: Gaining approval and avoiding rejection, pride in the importance of oneself in relationships.

Submission to a powerful other, then identifying with the other to avoid feeling depressed.

Concern about limited personal freedom.

Altering oneself to meet the needs of others.

Empathy with others' feelings; adapting to their wishes as a way of assuring their love.

Focus: Personal emphasis on privilege ("me first").

Couple emphasis on aggression/seduction.

Community emphasis on ambition.

Life Task: To move from dependence on approval to knowledge of personal strength to meet one's own needs. This usually requires personal loss. The resulting depression can lead to a more accurate self-assessment and understanding of tasks.

Top dogs require underdogs. Wherever a dominator model of society exists, there's a need for groups to dominate: South African blacks, women, factory workers, Japanese daughters-in-law, Third World countries skewing their own economies for the benefit of their dominant trading partners. They provide the services needed by the over-group. They are rewarded, at the very least, with continuing existence and, at most, with considerable unacknowledged power.

Acquiring the survival skills, insights and power of the dominated is what the TWO strategy is all about.

TWOS are helpers, out of touch with their own needs; they busy themselves meeting the needs of others. They want to get something from the people they are helping: attention, love, appreciation and dependency. They want to be needed. As children, TWOS learn to sacrifice their real feelings in order to please others. In return, they feel protected and approved.

> Jean's parents divorced when she was four. "They both needed me: Mother because I could get around my father and he would continue to support us, and my father because he was so lost."

TWOS show emotion so easily that it is difficult to realize that most of their feelings relate more to the moods and preferences of their relationship partners than to their own genuine reality. They are kind, sensitive and concerned for the good of others. They are self-sacrificing in their personal relationships. Warm, tactile persons who love to touch, they move out to others easily and make them comfortable. They are sympathetic and quick to notice what makes others feel important and nurtured.

However, TWOS expect others to notice what they are doing, and to respond in kind. "You should know what I need. I shouldn't have to ask!" is the unspoken assumption. If unnoticed, the TWO will probably feel upset and hurt, then quite possibly victimized and not appreciated for all he or she has done. A related problem occurs when the TWO gets close to doing or getting what she wants. Attention and recognition for service are not the real need. If she lets herself know what she wants and then does not get it, she will be miserable. Substituting attention to others' needs is easier to bear.

Parent-Child Issues

Children choose a TWO Program when they sense that their survival depends on meeting a parent's needs. They decide to take care of the parent, whether by becoming a helpful, pseudo-adult/pseudo-mother or, as with the hysteric, by acting out the parent's unconscious wishes and becoming a sexual tease. Either choice requires a tremendous concentration on the moods of others, a skill carried into later relationships.

The child acts in response to parental body language and tone of voice. He or she hears messages, whether voiced or unvoiced, which seem to say:

"Please me (take care of me)."

"Don't disagree with me."

"Don't think."

"Don't feel important."

The child's strategy is to survive through sensing what the powerful other person wants and altering him/herself to become or provide that want.

In later childhood, TWOS always focus their attention on what others want. They adapt themselves to others' emotional states, aiming to get close to the most popular or most powerful. Winning approval means being seen and noticed.

TWO behavior ranges from unconscious, severely disturbed forms through various degrees of conscious manipulation to a state of altruism. The distressed form, described in psychological literature as the hysteric, was one of the earliest noted by physicians of ancient Greece. The root meaning of the word hysterical, like hysterectomy, has to do with womb. Because physicians thought a "wandering womb" caused the symptoms, they named the disease "hysteria" and associated it primarily with women. We now know this is not true. Men also choose this Program.

Hysterics will often describe themselves as having been "father's favorite child," and sometimes the object of his sexual feelings. They describe their fathers as conflicted and full of contradictions, strongly instinctual, violent, impulsive, sometimes alcoholic, and on the other hand childish, soft, self-pitying and helpless. The hysteric grew up stuck in the conflict of repressing inner anger and needing outer approval.

Not all TWOS are hysterics, but the exaggerated process of the hysteric highlights the TWO pattern. Hysterics enlarge the culturally desired traits and mechanisms that characterize normal, vivacious sexuality—warmth, imagination and charm. They are exhibitionistic and self-dramatizing, and use language filled with superlatives. Strict adherence to the truth is not a concern if distortion will better serve the drama. Masochistic fantasies and promiscuity are not uncommon. TWOS act on impulse, substituting quick hunches and impressions for critical thought. They seem narcissistic, but their sense of safety and survival depends on the amount of attention they receive.

Although TWOS have real difficulty experiencing love and intimacy, their appearance is quite to the contrary. They are usually attractive because they do whatever is necessary to hold attention and approval. TWOS therefore are strongly interested in style and fashion, often appearing younger than their age. Their attention and warmth can delude one into feeling like an old friend, but closeness usually fails to develop. While hysterics look for emotional rapport, if they fail to receive it, they may blame the other for being boring or unresponsive, or show their sadness to make the other person feel guilty. A thin facade of self-confidence conceals self-doubt and uncertainty.

Hysterics seem unable to entertain themselves and require much attention from others. The problem is not boredom, but the premise of their Program that they need the other person's continued interest and affection to survive.

> Leah had such difficulty with menstruation that potent pain sedatives were prescribed when she was an early adolescent. In circumstantial detail, with spaces of painful, silent sobbing, she told her tale of addiction and medical mismanagement at the hands of a series of doctors, culminating in a hysterectomy at the age of 28.
>
> Only upon hearing the sad story for the third time, told with minor variations to an audience of rapt, sympathetic and indignant women, did her friend realize that while the story might have a core of truth, in reality Leah was presenting a victim drama.

The hysteric's defense mechanisms shift in response to social cues. The purpose of each defense is to prevent the awakening of repressed sexuality. Memory blanks and a lack of sexual feeling are clinical signs of repression. Fact and fantasy, blame and sadness intertwine to prevent a direct involvement with the world. Emotionality is a defense against deeper feelings and the dangers inherent in a real life.

The male hysteric also suffers sexual disturbance, potency problems, Don Juanism, conscious or unconscious homosexual fantasies, and often an intense, neurotic relationship with his mother.

Opposites attract. Hysterics and obsessive personalities (Enneagram ONE), who often marry, fall at opposite ends of the spectrum. The patterns close to consciousness in one type are deeply repressed in the other. Typically, neither partner recognizes the ONE's underlying passive dependency.

> After three years of marriage, Sandy saw her husband as a selfish, controlling tyrant who wanted to keep her a prisoner. Initially, it seemed like a storybook marriage. They were married just as she was beginning to be recognized as a talented sculptor and he had finished his medical training. He was proud of her attractiveness, seductive behavior and appeal to other men. He had never been with a woman quite so glamorous. However, he expected her to take care of him and manage the house according to his exacting specifications. He treated her more as an ideal and exclusive mother, who should gratify his sexual and dependency needs, while he remained passive.
>
> The marital conflicts were characteristic. Their courtship had been stormy, and marriage soon led to mutual disappointment. She blamed him for his cold detachment, miserliness and controlling attitudes. Her demanding behavior, extravagance and refusal to submit to his domination irritated him. He attempted to engage her through intellectual discussion and appeals to rational logic. She would respond initially, but then become emotional, displaying her anger or hurt feelings of rejection. He would then withdraw, feeling bewildered and frustrated, or erupt in rage.

Sandy, acting in the unconscious security-seeking mode of the TWO Program, had selected a man who would not desire her as a woman and an equal partner. She now had no choice in her strategy of continuing dependency other than to alternate between being his mother and his child.

The seductiveness attributed to TWOS comes from a desire to obtain approval, admiration and protection, rather than a feeling of intimacy or genital sexual pleasure. Seduction involves altering personal presentation in order to become desirable in one-to-one relationships. Physical closeness substitutes for emotional closeness.

Rivalry between TWOS is common. TWOS resent any competitive threat to the relationships they establish of possessive dependency with, and power over, their sexual partner. Initially, TWOS endow their partner with traits of an ideal, a father who will not make demands on them, but this changes to accord with their drama. Seducing other people through charm is challenging. If the other backs off, a TWO may pursue but then retreat in fear of rejection and entice the other into coming after him or her. Because she fears losing the partner, she often chooses a mate she can hold because of the other's dependency needs.

Ambition is the keynote of the TWO with a community focus. Association with and winning the approval of powerful others protects the TWO and assures privilege. The archetypal Shadow problem of pride, with its accompanying contempt for others, is felt acutely in this state. The power point of view is adopted without the assurance of its strength—a deadly position. Royal courtiers exemplify this sub-type description. An emphasis on "me first" also characterizes the personal mode. Aggressive maneuvering assures the TWO a share, and more, of whatever resources are available.

Revising the TWO Strategy

TWOS submit to and identify with someone who seems more powerful, able to protect them or to provide them with what they need. They repress needs that do not fit into the other person's life—one cause of depression. The other can also be a cause, a profession or an institution. Career fields such as nursing, social work, religious ministry and teaching traditionally attract TWOS and cultivate the TWO Program values. Most societies encourage a large proportion of their women to function as TWOS to husband and children.

Usually the loss of the addictive relationship, through divorce, death or some other mishap, precipitates the depression needed to change the TWO point of view. The temptation is to rush into another relationship rather than do the work of changing.

The spiritual and psychological task for TWOS is to start doing some things independently, to focus on being alone, and to get a sense of their personal needs. They need to notice when they replace real feelings with those designed to capture the attention of others. They have to stop depending on how others see them and develop a self that does not alter. A discipline of self-observation, art work, meditation and active imagination can help a sense of self gradually to emerge.

TWOS have to learn that they can get what they want without manipulating it through helpfulness *or* helplessness. They can say what they need and want. They can drop the games and truly protect themselves. TWOS need to recognize their real worth without swinging between self-important inflation and exaggerated humility.

Some behaviors, such as the use of flattery, indicate both rising anxiety and the desire to manipulate others through appearing helpless or "looking good." Having lived to please others for so long, TWOS will discover the fear of not owning a real self. To gain that sense of self, they need to acknowledge and take personal power in the family and such social institutions as neighborhood groups, unions, and professional associations.

Insecurity about surviving without others' protection and fear that independence will lead to never being loved can sabotage the emerging sense of real needs. TWOS need time to recognize and become familiar with their authentic feelings. A support group to "name" the experiences, discriminate the sources of social stress, and identify the steps of change can be helpful at this point.

Jungian psychotherapists symbolically describe many problems of the TWO strategy in the alchemical process of *Solutio*. Fixed, static aspects of the personality allow for no change. Transformation requires dissolution. The many forms of love and lust are agents in this process. Whatever, or whoever, is larger than the ego threatens to dissolve it. The TWO explores intense and ecstatic experiences rather than those with clear and structured meaning. The danger is to be swamped or drowned; the purpose is to survive with the unanswerable questions dissolved.

The unique values of the transcended TWO strategy are badly needed to bring balance to an increasingly ego-centric Western culture. Their grounded attention to the differently rhythmed developments and needs of each person around them, and an empathy which defuses conflict, are values we need to recognize, honor and support. Partnership rather than dominant power then becomes possible.

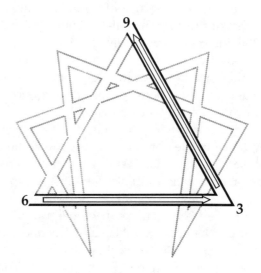

Point Three: The Program of Achievement with Emphasis on Image

Self-Definition: "I'm successful."
Shadow Issue: Lying
Rejected Element: Failure
Addiction: Efficiency
Strength Needed: Truth/hope
Defense Mechanism: Identification
Psychological Disturbance: Workaholism; manic-depression
Preoccupations Include: Identification with competitive achievement. Belief that they get love for what they produce rather than what they are.

Poor access to personal feelings.

Constant adjustment of image to gain approval. Self-deception to maintain a public image.

Identification of self with role or job over family concerns.

Submission by conforming to the other's values, then avoidance of depression by achieving the other's approval.

Convergent thinking: a multi-track mind focused on a single goal.
Focus: Personal emphasis on security.

Couple emphasis on masculinity/femininity.

Community emphasis on prestige.

Life Task: To stop valuing themselves in terms of their performance. Usually only a significant failure can precipitate the depression needed to sufficiently slow down and question what they are doing, and why. Hope comes with the practice of truth and in glimpsing a larger vision of lawfulness.

Fear and greed run the market economy, whose players are notorious for ignoring their feelings and any values other than the "bottom line" of profit. The business community is a natural arena for the THREE Program.

THREE is the Enneagram strategy which experiences the greatest difficulty with recognizing feelings, both one's own and those of others. It is a popular masculine strategy and American men in particular identify with its emphasis on aggressive competition, efficiency and an image of success. This type of personality is also emerging strongly among some women as they move into the business world. THREES identify with success; they tend to put their whole worth as individuals into the achievements and roles they most value. They organize and carefully plan their lives and contacts to attain their goals.

The type is highly prized throughout American culture. THREES identify with the images most valued: youth, energy, competition and achievement.

The rewards are high. The excitement and rush of energy feel great, and THREES are materially rewarded with prestige, money and power. They know how to turn on the adrenalin, but the physical cost can also be high. One woman, returning from a ski vacation with a fractured knee, did not take time from work to visit a doctor— "there was so much work to be caught up." She developed an infection and almost lost her leg.

Parent-Child Issues

A THREE grows up with a parent who consistently pushes the child to achieve ("Make me proud of you!"), who fails to be pleased ("5 A's and a B—why isn't it 6 A's?"), who fails to notice accomplishment, or who expects the child to succeed in areas of the parent's interests. This places the child in a dilemma. The parent's messages seem to be:

"Be a winner."
"Don't feel your feelings."
"Try to please me."
"Try harder."

When children receiving these messages do not fulfill the parent's demands, they feel unacceptable, but satisfactory performance is open-ended, so nothing they do ever seems enough. They have to keep going and try harder. One woman connected these feelings in childhood with the thought: "They'd tell me they loved me if I were good enough, wouldn't they? I never felt anything I did was enough, so I'd do more—painting, skating, dancing, playing music, joining the swim team. When I grew up, I just translated this into taking on more projects."

There are other costs: suppressed feelings of not participating in life or having genuine emotional experiences, and of doing a good job without feeling good about it.

The strategy is to find activities and attributes that the child decides will win the widest possible approval. The child creates his or her image with these qualities to avoid the sense of being unacceptable.

Those who choose a THREE Program often become managers or administrators, and they insist on their own type of performance from others. They are demanding, and have a hard time understanding inefficiency, incompetence or any waste of time. They want clear goals and evaluations. Since the success of their enterprise is all-important in their eyes and they are willing to sacrifice time, family, and other interests, they expect others to make similar sacrifices. They rarely acknowledge the almost constant feeling of being tired and overspent as the years go on.

Projecting a public image of success is almost as important as the work they are doing. Just as they dress for success, THREES put on feelings they see as appropriate. THREES are adaptable negotiators and problem solvers, though not on a feeling level. Any personal feelings that make them uncomfortable or queasy are put aside to be thought about later, if ever.

THREES give themselves little private or personal life. They get caught up in their roles and what they are trying to gain. In Jungian terms, they identify with their personas, wearing public masks which portray their roles but do not allow them to be known or know themselves.

> Laura, an MBA with a flourishing career, began to panic when she approached 40. She had not had time to have a baby in the rush of accomplishing her career goals. A first marriage after she finished college ended when she accepted an executive position with a new company on the West Coast and her husband decided not to accompany her.
>
> Now she was in a relationship with the CEO of her corporation and he wanted a child. Laura wanted this man and thought having a child would be a marvelous new experience, but she

was aware that her body was aging. She was caught between conflicting images of what she wanted and possibilities that might have been. She did not know how to connect with her ambivalent feelings about bearing a child.

THREES like to run their own shows and often overlook what others contribute to the success of their work or professions. They may manipulate others, either to get the work done or use as stepping stones to the next success. The pattern from childhood continues. No one victory ever seems enough to assure them of their essential worth. They must do more.

Achievement brings attention. For the social sub-type, prestige and a full schedule are the answer. Emotions are subordinated while action takes the foreground. But paradoxically, their triumphs are inwardly directed toward gaining love.

> Barry was the third of four brothers; he decided early that he was not going to be lost in the shuffle. His parents carried a heavy social life and, in their rounds of business entertaining, scarcely seemed to have time for the boys, who grew up under the care of a series of live-in housekeepers. Barry competed with his brothers for recognition so that, when he entered grammar school, he already knew how to command adult attention.
>
> His parents' recognition felt like love, and he could get attention for performance. However, the message he still heard was, "You can do more and do better." Who he was and how he felt were largely ignored. He became addicted to prestige. He stayed away from hurt, anger and warfare with his parents by taking extracurricular school activities for which he wanted and received thanks and recognition. Not doing a good job would have damaged his self-esteem, so he continued collecting credentials, involving himself with more and more activities, always trying harder.
>
> Barry's parents placed emphasis on winning and identification with job, task, mask, or image. He bought their Program and developed a fear of stopping, of not having a project, of not having attention.

Community-focused THREES enjoy conversation and know how to keep their audience's attention. They emphasize what will please others; they play whatever role will impress the group at hand. One THREE explained, "It's a matter of constantly adjusting to the audience. It's an evolving image."

The sexual self-image of the THREE includes fantasy elements. The couple focus emphasizes attributes of masculinity and femininity which promise, "I'll be what you want me to be." The degree of others' regard becomes the gauge for behavior: put something out, get feedback, adjust; project an image but don't respect those who buy it. "I can please and amuse you guys and you don't even know who I am." Intimacy is a wild card and they handle it gingerly. There is an element of competition and performance even in lovemaking. Sexuality confuses them and they prefer to protect themselves from anxiety by retreating from intimacy, placing low priority on relationships.

THREES don't present their emotions. It bothers them to let in another person's feelings or get in touch with their own. They do not relax; they are not empathetic. They are uneasy with emotions in others and avoid uneasiness by introducing diverting activities. THREES can't stand a non-verbal space for too long because their feelings may surface, so they avoid the "now" and fantasize about the future.

Money and ownership of material goods provide some security for THREE's survival concerns, but no matter how much they have, there is always the possibility of some disaster occuring for which they will not have enough. Their drive to acquire more continues, interlaced with self-deception. For example, Jean expressed her concern:

> "Sam's business clears $80,000 a year but we live like we're making $180,000. I've always enjoyed our lifestyle but we've refinanced the house three times in the last ten years. He has so many lines of credit, the bankers can't keep track. He says I'll be a rich widow, but I'm tired of co-signing loans. Any extra money I get simply disappears into his money machine. What are we living for anyway?" Sam protested sadly that Jean didn't believe in him anymore, and he needed her belief so that he could continue his highwire financial juggling. He discounted her judgment because she had no direct experience of the business world: "She is plainly not objective; you can tell by how emotional she is," a response that infuriated her because her feelings did not invent the facts she perceived.
>
> Sam wanted Jean to believe that he was building his financial empire for her and the family, not for his own ego and power needs. He expected her to show her loyalty by co-signing new loans "without sabotaging questions." He expected her to stall creditors and use her executive talents in his interests. For many years, the portion of truth in what he said, his affection and his physical attraction to her obscured for both of them his ego-centric manipulations.

The psychological disorder associated with the THREE Program is type A behavior of workaholism and, in extreme form, manic depression. The THREE's defense mechanism of choice is identification.

In the outer world, the dark side of the THREE Program is most evident in those systems which substitute the aggressive presentation of an image for the truth: for example, in hard-sell campaigns, whether for products or politicians. The telephone company which tells us to "reach out and touch someone" misappropriates a reality of human intimacy for its own profit. Efficiency, skill and self-serving propaganda also govern THREE group behavior.

Revising the THREE Strategy

This strategy normally changes only with failure. Challenge at the personal and group levels is necessary for THREES to recognize something is wrong. The way out of their dilemma is to slow down and ask what's going on. Who are they trying to please and why? What do they want? What do their feelings tell them about personal desires that have little to do with what is popular and public?

THREES can be in a state of pain for a long time and not admit it, as long as they are productive. They have to begin to notice how they keep slipping away from feelings and that they have no experience of a range of emotions. They need someone who will hang in with them, tell the truth, and demand it from them. This can be a therapist, but is more often a marriage partner.

The words "image," "appearance" and "outwardly" are crucial to understanding the THREE's Shadow issue of deceit. While they seem to lack much drive to *be* good, they intensely desire to *appear* good. That is the lie, designed not so much to deceive others as to deceive themselves. They cannot, or will not, tolerate the pain of self-reproach.[1]

Deceit, including self-deceit, pervades all image-making. Everything that does not fit has to be hidden. THREES have an investment in representing the facts of their lives in a particular light. The other person's "consent" confirms this and avoids "loss of face." The partner who attempts to live with a THREE is often in the position of doubting his or her own perceptions and judgments, because the THREE employs a variety of techniques and power tactics to demand loyalty and support.

The middle-years-marriage phenomenon, in which one partner reluctantly "wakes up," often precipitates a depression. It can be the beginning of personal individuation for both partners, but it is rough work with much temptation to turn back. The couple may have lived for years within a set of agreements based on a lie, an unreal, inauthentic definition of their reality.

When the THREE's partner begins to reconnect with the truth of their plight, he or she must state it to save his own sanity and not defend his point of view in terms of the THREE's system of thought. He must stay with his own perceptions, judgments and decisions. Only in this way can the relationship revive—and the THREE begin to heal.

Undoubtedly, persons other than THREES can live a lie. The THREE's investment in—and seduction by—image makes this strategy particularly vulnerable to deceit. The business world, particularly advertising, public relations and media work, attracts THREES and fertilize their values.

The alchemical term *Nigrado* (blackness) describes some aspects of the spiritual aspects of the THREE program, specifically the lack of relationship between achievement and feeling. This has to be restructured.[2]

THREES need to revise their life strategy to include goals other than winning, the source of the distortion. They need to stop their incessant activity and admit perceptions from within and outside their bodies. They need to work to amplify and use their emotional and instinctual responses.

The mature THREE strategy, a productive, creative, high-energy Program, is of great value to society, but THREES need to recognize that it is neither the central value nor the only life worth living.

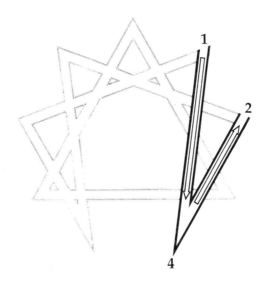

Point Four: The Program of Excellence with Moody Nostalgia

Self-Definition: "I'm unique. I conform to standards of excellence."
Shadow Issue: Envy
Rejected Element: The "commonplace"
Addiction: Superior standards with contempt for lesser standards
Strength Needed: Contentment
Defense Mechanism: Introjection, artistic sublimation
Psychological Disturbance: Depression and manic-depression
Preoccupations Include: Attraction to the distant and unavailable.

Attachment to a melancholy mood, impatience with flat ordinary feelings, need to re-intensify through loss, fantasy and drama.

Submission to loss and limitation by making a transformed version.

Luxury and artistic good taste as bolsters to self-esteem.

Push-pull attention focus on negative features of what one has and positive features of what is not available, reinforcing feelings of abandonment and loss but also fostering sensitivity to emotion and pain in others with ability to support them in crisis.

Focus: Personal emphasis on reckless, defensive action.

Couple emphasis on competition.

Community emphasis on shame.

Life Task: To achieve a sense of the reality of now and to attain the strength of contentment and balance in harmony with all that is. Uncovering the grief and sadness under the creative displacement allows completion.

A fascination with death, the transitory nature of life and beauty, supplies the impetus for tragic drama and much great poetry. Those who author such works are often FOURS, for the particular bias of the FOUR strategy develops as a transformation of tragedy.

FOURS consider themselves to be quite different from other people. They avoid a sense of ordinariness, but are disturbed that others seem to possess what they are missing in their own lives. Every FOUR has suffered, or identified with, an early childhood loss. Often FOURS attribute their differentness to this tragic beginning of their lives. They have gone through loneliness and suffering that others can't understand.

> Liz grew up as the oldest of three girls. Her father deserted the family when she was barely seven. Her mother, addicted to gambling, lived in a fantasy world of constant expectations of "making it big" and changing their life around. In the meantime, they lived in a series of boarding houses around Reno while the mother worked as a cocktail waitress and entered a series of abusive relationships. Liz, an attractive child with a huge smile, determined to survive and ingratiated herself with neighbors who helped her with food and protection when needed. She was also bright enough to win recognition and attention at school.

Parent-Child Issues

The child learns early that his or her parents are not available to give emotional support. The messages he or she picks up include:

"Don't count on my being here for you."

"Don't be close."

(sometimes:) "Don't feel what you feel; feel what I feel (sad)."

FOURS desire to feel the happiness that others seem to enjoy, but since the original source of happiness is an abandoning parent, they associate happiness with disappointment. Any happiness triggers the core fear of abandonment. Intimacy is dangerous, and when it is felt, anger surfaces. A FOUR wishes to reject first rather than chance rejection and re-abandonment. "The other is going to leave anyway. Nothing I can do will make any difference. It is better at least to feel somewhat in charge, that I'm making it happen."

The child develops the FOUR strategy to prevent the immobilizing depression experienced with actual loss. Thereafter, he or she avoids total emotional involvement in any current relationship. After the real loss, the child fills his or her life with imagination and fantasy, explores symbolic interpretations of what happened, and plays at the edge of his desire, to be close—and to be destroyed.

There is a difference between depression (lack of ability to find a way to act) and melancholia (sad/sweet cycling of thought). Depression is circumstantial, immobilizing, painful and full of self-hatred. Abandonment, loss of relationship or loss of power can trigger it. The child, in choosing a FOUR Program, moves from the depression of real loss to a state of melancholy and moody nostalgia. Here, death and loss are not totally unattractive; they become intertwined with fantasies—"How wonderful it would be if only . . ."

The desired melancholic mood often involves a drama, with a tragic hero or heroine experiencing absence or loss. FOURS enjoy living not in the moment but in imagination. They often use their understanding of symbolic expression in poetry, music, art, creative writing or acting. Their work is original and serious. They are also creative in shaping their immediate environment, with a sense of what is beautiful, elegant and tasteful.

Unaffected, spontaneous behavior is difficult for a FOUR; wariness is natural. FOURS tend to rehearse how they want to appear before others. They long for casual simplicity but never seem to attain it. They have an air about them that says they are special and that they understand things better than other people do. Even their body language says they believe themselves to have more taste, style and deep feelings than others. They are often understated but elegant in dress. Their style comes from their special understanding and use of symbols.

FOURS envy others who seem more natural than they do. Feelings of any kind absorb their attention. They pick over the sadnesses of their past, the lost opportunities, the hurt, loneliness and abandonment caused by others. Memories don't make demands the way current relationships do; FOURS enjoy the sense of longing for what was or could have been. These longings animate the richly sensual world of their imagination, a highly addictive state of consciousness that they resist giving up.

They sabotage their own completion and successes. They don't allow things to finish before they take on something else. There is a sweetness in longing they do not find in possession. "I can't have it, and I must have it." They are good at carrying torches and being alone. They feel unworthy to have what they want.

They are attractive, often charming people but their readiness to flee makes intimacy difficult. They do not invite closeness; they are not interested in mutuality and equality. FOURS are not easily pleased and any routine is boring. When they seem easy to get along with, they may be feeling indifferent.

They have compassion; they know pain and may have great sensitivity to hurts that others might not even notice. Liz, the abused child mentioned earlier, became an extraordinarily creative woman and used her knowledge of childhood loss in a career as a political advocate for children.

Intimacy is stronger at a distance for FOURS. They hold themselves back from what they want, which increases their longing. In relationships, FOURS are elitists and tend to see the bad when they're here and the good when they're afar. They want to change the other person into the epitome of what the other should be. FOURS find it difficult to deal with "warts and all," and they tend to let relationships fade. They appreciate pursuit as long as they don't feel manipulated.

FOURS are competitive, without needing to win all the time. Rather, competition is a means to measure their worth against others, or what others have, pointing back to the original question, "Why was I abandoned?"

Their Shadow trait is envy, combined with sadness. Their self-esteem hangs on some outer gauge and their attention is constantly directed to what is absent. The defense mechanism associated with this Program is introjection, and the mental disorder is depression or manic-depression. There are physical dysfunctions as well. FOURS seem to be disproportionately represented among anorexics and bulimics, diseases symbolically associated with hunger and longing.

In the Program variations of Chart 4, each focal point intensifies some dangerous personal feeling. FOURS like living on the edge. The couple focus is competition, to prove one's worth and not be underestimated. Shame drives the communal question of measuring up to standards. A recklessness about personal survival recreates the possibility of loss for the self-preservation sub-type.

FOURS submit to the reality of what has happened to them—the loss and the limitation—but they avoid the devastation of despair. They reconstruct their experiences using symbolic fantasy and substitute the milder depression of melancholy. In the outer world, something similar happens as displaced people avoid demoralization and attempt to cope with destruction. Among groups dominated by the FOUR strategy, the Irish during the period of English oppression stand out for developing a rich literature of poetry, plays and novels. In the United States, soul music, gospel singing and the blues tradition transform the unspeakable group tragedy of slavery and racism. Refugees, displaced persons throughout the world and victims of the Holocaust breed similar casts of mind.

Revising the FOUR Strategy

Moving from a FOUR Program requires the risk of attachment and caring. FOURS must bring themselves into the present; they must stop their escape from a flawed reality into idealized fantasy. When they enter therapy, they need to have their emotions taken seriously, without the therapist over-empathizing with their depression or drama. They need to notice how they sabotage their personal work. Instead of dealing with their own needs, identifying their own Shadow tendencies and concretely changing their actions, they prefer to focus attention on envious comparisons. They concentrate on rejecting others or how others misunderstand them. Questions of competition and shame distract them from the difficult work at hand.

The Shadow issue of envy lies in its corrosive ability to destroy existing sensitivity and contentment. FOURS need to learn contentment in relationships by seeing both the good and the bad in the moment.

At a community level, the difficulty with a FOUR group strategy is its tendency to fail to mobilize power to make change possible. Levers for change are at hand. For instance, community organizing builds on small experiences of group success to develop larger changes; its organizing tactics can develop and allow FOURS' creativity to flourish.

As they move from their self-constrictions, FOURS bring a rich understanding of what the alchemists called *Mortificatio*, which can help others know their yearnings and the transformative possibilities in their pain. Theodore Roethke's remarkable poem *In a Dark Time* describes this process. He begins with the necessity of facing the darkness: "In a dark time, the eye begins to see, / I meet my shadow in the deepening shade..." He concludes with the experience of completion: "A fallen man, I climb out of my fear. / The mind enters itself, and God the mind, / And one is One, free in the tearing wind."[3]

In this poem, the darkness opens a new vision. The ego's desires are overthrown and the unconscious erupts, as nature and animal, into consciousness. Roethke explores the madness we experience when the inner and outer world intertwine, the opposites come into view, and we walk the narrow edge between them. Transpersonal meaning shines through his powerful images. From the depths comes illumination into the greater meaning of existence.

A Summary of the Submission and Depression Response Group

As a child, the TWO's strategy is to survive through sensing what the powerful other person wants and altering him/herself to become or provide that want.

THREES' childhood strategy is to find activities and attributes that the child decides will win the widest possible approval. The child creates his or her image with these qualities to avoid the sense of being unacceptable.

The child develops the FOUR strategy to prevent the immobilizing depression experienced with actual loss. Thereafter, he or she avoids total emotional involvement in any current relationship. After the real loss, the child fills his or her life with imagination and fantasy, explores symbolic interpretations of what happened, and plays at the edge of his desire, to be close—and to be destroyed.

TWO

Life Script Program: Helpfulness with manipulation
Self-definition/self-image: "I'm helpful."
Shadow issue: Parasitic Pride
Rejected transformation element: One's own needs
Addiction: Service/manipulation
Virtue/strength needed: Appropriate self-value (Humility)
Defense mechanism: Repression
Psychological disturbance: Hysteria/dependent personality

THREE

Life Script Program: Efficiency with emphasis on image
Self-definition/self-image: "I'm successful."
Shadow issue: Lying
Rejected transformation element: Failure
Addiction: Efficiency
Virtue/strength needed: Truth/hope
Defense mechanism: Identification
Psychological disturbance: Workaholic (Type A personality);
    manic-depression

FOUR

Life Script Program: Excellence with moody nostalgia
Self-definition/self-image: "I'm unique. I conform to elite standards."
Shadow issue: Envy
Rejected transformation element: The "commonplace"
Addiction: Superior standards with contempt for lesser
Strength/virtue needed: Contentment
Defense mechanism: Introjection, artistic sublimation
Psychological disturbance: Depression and manic-depression

Chapter Two:

The Programs of Anxiety and Flight

The Program of Knowledge with Withdrawal
The Program of Security with Fear and Doubt
The Program of Easy Optimism with Uneasy Activity

Photo by Michelle Vignes

A deer, hearing the sound of a distant hunter, freezes for a moment, then bounds away in terror. Humans can react in similar ways to danger, stopping breathing, going silent, then fleeing. But to experience a state of high alertness in a body prepared for action is also to feel alive. Anxiety merges with excitement. We cultivate the edge of terror, scaring ourselves with horror movies, roller coaster rides, sexual games and taking chances.

A certain degree of anxiety helps to prepare change. For example, stage fright releases excitement that can charge the subsequent performance with emotional energy. We fear heights and depths, emptiness and "not knowing." Our fear, if it is not overwhelming, alerts us to what is needed and stretches our capacity to cope with two kinds of anxiety—one, not having the required knowledge to deal with a situation and the other, a fear of the unknown itself.

We fear death; we fear what we don't want to see; we often fear our own anger, which we project and experience as if it were coming from others. Anxiety intertwines with self-image. We fear being thought a fool and having to admit that we don't know the answers. Paradoxically, only in going to that place of unknowing can we break free from fear. The normal response to fear is flight. Our task is often to sustain ourselves in the face of our fear and to move through it to another reality.

Program FIVE, withdrawing, setting boundaries, using camouflage; Program SIX, with heightened alertness and flight or counter-phobic aggression; program SEVEN, using diversion—all work to avoid fear. Release requires facing the fears in a different way.

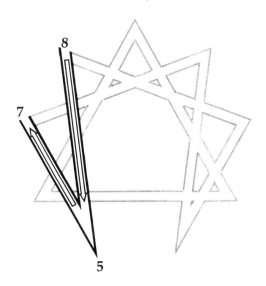

Point Five: The Program of Knowledge with Withdrawal

Self-Definition: "I'm perceptive."

Shadow Issue: Miserliness

Rejected Element: Meaninglessness

Addiction: Knowledge

Strength Needed: Detachment

Defense Mechanism: Isolation (compartmentalization)

Psychological Disturbance: Avoidant personality

Preoccupations Include: Concern with privacy; withdrawal; social/anti-social dichotomy.

Restricting and minimizing personal needs as a way of non-involvement. Need to control unpredictable feelings and reactions.

Sectioning off emotionally charged experiences into predetermined time units; setting boundaries.

Interest in using analytical knowledge as a substitute for emotional experience.

Confusion between spiritual non-attachment and personal withdrawal from emotional pain.

"Outside observer" point of view leading some to feel isolated from the events of one's own life and others to a point of view detached from the biases of personal fear or desire.

Focus: Personal emphasis on "home as castle."

Couple emphasis on confidence.

Community emphasis on totems, identifying with "those who know."

Life Task: Gaining knowledge of life by stepping into action from being an observer, taking in exactly what is needed and letting the rest go.

A certain proportion of men and women have always felt a need to live their lives apart from community. Not only hermits, but many others feel the need for vast amounts of solitude. Some have demanding work to do; others seem to fear the invasions of the outer world as a personal threat.

Parent-Child Issues

As children, FIVES develop a strategy of withdrawal from parents they perceive as either intrusive or emotionally depriving. Parents convey a danger in being close or belonging, and the child translates this into an instruction:

"Don't be close."

"Don't belong."

> Peg's mother prided herself on her red hair and violent temper. She ran the show, not only for her husband and children, but also for her own mother, many brothers, and, on occasion, for neighbors as well. She regarded Peg, her daughter from an earlier marriage, as her private property through whom she could reclaim the opportunities she had missed in life.
>
> In thinking back to her childhood, Peg later said there was no aspect of her life that her mother did not invade. Even unexpressed feelings seemed transparent to her mother. "Wipe that look off your face! What do you mean by looking at me like that!" Peg learned to bury herself in books and fantasies, altering the endings of her favorite stories. Her earliest favorite stories had to do with magical invisibility, which she rehearsed with great satisfaction en route to school and back. Of course she never shared her thoughts, even with her brothers.

Sometimes deprivation involves physical dislocations, which prevent the child from putting down roots. Peg's parents not only moved often; when she displeased them, they also threatened to send her away to boarding school and summer camp as punishment.

Such children withdraw into a world of information, imaginative thought and reflection. The determined pursuit of privacy allows them to survive and leads them to self-sufficiency and resourcefulness. Competition, prestige and success do not attract them. Even living habits, eating and drinking are kept on a scale that does not require too much time or energy.

The child decides that people threaten something essential to her survival. She develops a protective strategy of playing possum, camouflaging her existence and reducing her needs to a minimum so that she becomes as unnoticeable as possible. She then discovers that she can pursue her own interests undisturbed.

FIVES need the opportunity to reconstruct the facts of reality into an intelligible pattern. As loners on the edge of events, they observe life rather than participate in it. They take pains to know what is going on but not to be involved.

The reserve and non-commitment of FIVES can be difficult. They tend to forget names and are uncomfortable with the small talk of social gatherings, which makes them feel drained and empty. They often leave parties unobtrusively without saying goodbye. Time is precious to them, and if a thing is not useful, they see no reason to waste their time on it. On the other hand, in a focused conversation, they are sensitive listeners. Everything interests them, and they are not judgmental. They often have unexpected depths of knowledge tucked away on a wide range of subjects.

When asked what they feel, however, they will probably answer with what they think. An urgent emotional difficulty calls out a prompt response, but they may realize their feelings only later when they think about the event. They enjoy intimacy when it is free from threats of dependency.

> Tim: "People never get all of me, only what I can handle giving. I like being pursued rather than pursuing, but I want my partner to respect my time and privacy. It takes time to figure out how I feel about this other person. When problems occur I can always say, 'To hell with this, I can live alone.' However, I don't want to, not completely."

Abstract models of human behavior, systems and theories intrigue FIVES. Others often assume they replace their feelings with a scheme of ideas about what one is supposed to feel. Actually, emotions are not of primary interest to them. They use knowledge to reduce their anxiety about being drawn into potentially disturbing situations where they may have no control. Their internal defense mechanism is isolation; they suspend the flow of feelings while they observe and decide what to do.

FIVES appear to be stingy with their time, money and knowledge. They guard their time and privacy. They seldom think that what they know is sufficiently comprehensive and complete to be worth saying. An ascetic and minimalist lifestyle requires exacting economies in order to remain independent. When they feel a strong desire for something, however, they become absorbed in getting it.

In a one-to-one relationship, the couple focus often achieves the freest FIVE lifestyle. After surviving the testing of boundaries, relationships are characteristically confident. In relationships, as in other interests, FIVES are either totally involved or totally detached. They want other people to see only what they put out, not who they really are. For the FIVE whose primary instinct is personal survival in deeper isolation, the home is a secure refuge with its control of private, personal space. The communal FIVE tends to seek out "totems"—source people in his field of interest, the inner circle of thinkers who influence others. However, even here the relationship can carry its own FIVE hallmarks:

> Peg, in her need to understand her family's machinations, became fascinated with psychology. After finishing her scholastic work, she sought out the founders of psychological systems for personal study. As she mastered each system, each guru in turn assumed her discipleship because she asked intelligent questions, understood the principles, and never disagreed with any point of the teaching. She had a sense of humor and could use and teach the material with style.
>
> The gurus were wrong about her discipleship, however. She simply did not consider it important to share her points of disagreement with them. This also prevented any emotional encounter.

FIVES consider themselves discerning. They seem compelled to avoid feelings of emptiness by filling themselves with knowledge. They fear the void and do not want to face the dread it arouses. They are drawn to wisdom, but since it takes much time to become wise, they are always preparing themselves so that what they eventually express will be well thought out. Endless preparation is an addictive state of consciousness, and they are reluctant to give this up.

What goes on in their privacy is thought. They avoid distractions, and they use their time to review projects in detail, to prepare mentally for things they will encounter in the future, and to go over old events. Privacy sustains them and allows them to produce, which connects them to the world. Although they appear to be highly independent, FIVES are very attuned to what others want. They provide it in order to buy privacy. FIVES can be unexpectedly witty and laugh at almost anything. They are prone to magical thinking, warding off dangers by indirect means and charting the waters ahead of time.

Groups which attract FIVES and hold their values include monasteries and academic faculties.

Revising the FIVE Strategy

Growth for the FIVE involves "going public," sharing themselves and their knowledge with other people. FIVES need additional information, personal contact and grounding in reality. They need to take back the experiences of others into their privacy, and (a counter-phobic reason) they need to go to the danger that stimulates fear and seek real communication about things that matter in the outer world. They need to risk sharing their incomplete knowledge and thereby find that it can become a way of dialoguing, building onto insights in community with other people.

The Shadow issue of a miser is possessiveness. What FIVES seek can vary from material goods and power (Howard Hughes) to knowledge (Faust). Once acquired, it is held for personal use, not for sharing. Grasping denies both the value of community and the intrinsic meaning of the desired object. The root meaning of money as exchange is lost. People often fail to notice money's power to transform them. Those who set out to acquire wealth fashion their lives in such a way that they are significantly changed before they reach that goal. For FIVES, disclosure of their use of money can increase consciousness.

When FIVES recognize their habitual detachment from feelings, they can begin to place themselves in situations where people can draw them out. In therapy or self-observation practices, FIVES need to bring awareness of feelings back into the present moment and risk more self-disclosure. FIVES' life task is to gain a more direct knowledge of life by living it and by moving from observing to participating. They have to take what they need before withdrawing.

FIVES must try to recognize when they use data gathering to delay action and when they replace emotions with analysis. Once, when Peg was doing a group analysis, one of her mentors halted the verbal flow with a kiss. She responded, then finished her sentence. The group laughed, and she finally understood that her feelings always took second place to her thinking. Gestalt, body work and art methods which emphasize the now are helpful and allow the FIVE time to connect emotions with insight.

FIVES need to see their tendencies to withdraw from intensity and commitment, to withhold and censor comments, and to compartmentalize their lives. They need to notice their fear of emotion and their resistance to achieve a more complete self-knowledge. At some point they have to stop gathering information and face their inner emptiness. They have to follow T.S. Eliot's advice in *East Coker*:

> In order to arrive at what you do not know
> > You must go by a way which is the way of ignorance.
> In order to possess what you do not possess
> > You must go by the way of dispossession.[1]

The FIVE talent for discrimination and boundary drawing allows an intense awareness of opposites. Psychological growth requires that the tension of opposing feelings be contained until a third point of deeper consciousness is reached. In the alchemical symbols for psychological development, *Separatio* ushers in conscious existence, the separation of subject from object, the "I" from the "not-I." To the extent a person remains unconscious, he identifies with one of the two. For example he may see himself as generous without being aware of his greed. As FIVES become conscious, they are able to sustain and endure the internal opposites, without projecting one of the pair onto an outer "enemy." The detached objectivity of the evolved FIVE strategy becomes possible.

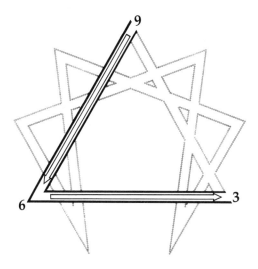

Point Six: The Program of Security with Fear and Doubt

Self-Definition: "I'm loyal. I'm cautious."
Shadow Issue: Cowardice or counter-phobic reckless courage
Rejected Element: Originality
Addiction: Security
Strength Needed: Courage (Faith)
Defense Mechanism: Projection
Psychological Disturbance: Anxiety disorder, paranoid schizophrenia
Preoccupations Include: High alertness to danger.

Phobic/counter-phobic authority problems; submit or rebel; push or surrender.

Identity with the underdog.

Procrastination; thinking replaces doing.

Amnesia regarding success and pleasure.

Suspicion of other's motives, fear of hostility and possible eruption of one's own negative reactions.

Skepticism and doubt.

Scanning the environment to look for clues that might explain inner sense of threat.

Focus: Personal emphasis on warmth/affection.

Couple emphasis on strength/beauty.

Community emphasis on duty.

Life Task: To achieve faith that nothing from the outside can hurt his or her essence; to attain trust and strength of courage.

"Fear...is the beginning of wisdom."[2] Wariness, the ability to focus on what is *out there,* is essential for survival. Just as an animal stops all motion while scanning for danger, a SIX has a similar sense of danger and often suspends activity for a state of high alertness.

The SIX point on the Enneagram represents the strategy with the greatest difficulty in doing and in taking credit for what one has done. However, SIXES usually have a highly developed emotional intelligence. They are in touch with their own and others' feelings. Danger is here, but also intimacy.

Parent-Child Issues

Some children are preoccupied with what is permitted, okay and safe—and what is not. They experience strong fear. They grow up convinced there is not enough love around to protect them. Either they avoid the frightening aspects of life, or they react counterphobicly and place themselves in maximum danger so they might know what terrifies them and figure out what to do about it. They seem to live their lives as if they were constantly responding to parental directives:

"Don't do."

"Be careful."

"Don't make it. Don't succeed."

"Don't be important."

"Don't outshine your parents."

"If you don't watch out, it'll/I'll get you."

Some children don't accept these messages of worthlessness. They respond to their circumstances with anger.

> Eric grew up under the harsh discipline and tremendous performance expectations of his musician father. By the age of 14, he had performed in many of the great concert halls of this country and abroad. He had also been physically and sexually abused by his father, a fact he could not share with those around him. By the time he was able to establish himself on his own, he had a reputation for drug abuse and physical violence.
>
> He was constantly at odds with authority. He made it a point to find out who was in charge so he could undermine them. He went against any rules or structures that he encountered. He opposed not only concert managers but also his financial backers, record companies and others necessary to his career.
>
> This behavior accomplished two things: it provided an outlet for his anger, and it guaranteed that he would not achieve the

success that his talent justified and which had seemed so important to his father. Success terrified him. He did not believe in his talent. Success meant he was like his father, a comparison he emotionally rejected.

SIXES constantly prepare for action, then vacillate. They identify with underdogs, fighting the rest of society. Even those not as disturbed as Eric find it hard to handle success. Damage to a child's sense of self-esteem can occur at any level of society. When social and economic pressures reinforce it, the effects can be devastating. These systematically intimidated children are suspicious, particularly of anyone proposing to do good things for them. They do not fall for scams. Lack of information, hidden agendas, secrecy and not being aboveboard are all red flags, signaling hidden motives, meanings and purposes.

SIXES' strategy is to focus on danger, to scan the environment for all possible threats and to program their behavior to avoid them. An alternative, if they can muster the strength, is to meet danger head on and defuse it.

The SIX learns to live with—and use—apprehension and fear.

SIXES believe in authority. They have a great need, for their own security, to know what is right and wrong, codified in the rules and documents of an institution (e.g., the Law, the Church, the Armed Forces). But then their attention switches from an impulse to act to an opposite position of intense internal questioning. Their doubt delays their taking action and allays the fear of punishment for questioning authority that they experienced as children.

> Elena grew up in a WASP suburb, never quite feeling she fit in. Her Latin father ran a successful trucking business and was widely regarded as having mob connections. Nevertheless, he had money and insisted that his children go to the best schools. Elena's Anglo mother "crawled into a bottle after giving birth to five children in less than ten years," and Elena, the second child but oldest girl, cared for the others as best she could. Her father, who always seemed in a rage, terrified and angered her, and she felt helpless and unprotected by her mother. She obeyed and made herself as unattractive as possible, "snuffly-nosed, teary and very overweight."
>
> Growing up, she became the "perfect preppy," fulfilling her father's expectations, but she had no sense of what she should do with her life. "The Sixties were great. In college, I found anti-establishment causes to identify with and everyone was with me. It was a great time for ethnic roots. However, I couldn't settle on a major study."

Focused on personal security, she found that the warmth and affection of friends gave meaning to her life. She drifted into a public health career, but she had no goals of personal or professional success. Her sexual life was always as part of a triad with another man and woman, both of whom regarded her as their "best and closest friend." She recognized that in this way she was close to whatever terrified her, but she also avoided it.

SIXES identify with group norms and feel themselves most alive when they belong to a specific group which commands their loyalty. However, they often sense the group making great demands on them.

SIXES observe others closely with a skilled imagination. They are remarkably astute. Sometimes, however, they overlook the obvious. SIXES watch for threats to their group's well-being and for any deviations from rules and norms. When they break the rules, they cannot admit it to themselves, so they use projection and denial as defense mechanisms. The psychological stress associated with this type is paralyzing doubt; the mental disorder is paranoid schizophrenia, a state similar to that captured by the image of the breakdown of the computer HAL 2000 in the movie *2001*.

The SIX who is focused on community and preoccupied with duty obeys the rules without open challenge. In childhood, a demanding parent reinforced respect for authority. Attending school meant conforming to the authority of the teacher and to an internal injunction, "to obey, not to decide." Outside authorities make the decisions. Boundary questions (Who belongs and who does not? Who has power over me, and who do I outrank?) were and remain important to SIXES.

Leisure poses a problem, but so does taking any initiative in their own interest. They are natural group members. They like the feeling of solidarity and support. Police, military and religious groups often have a SIX character. By and large, SIXES are not "self-starters." By avoiding risk, they lose many opportunities. Insecurity can cause them to consider any opposition, or even difference of opinion, dangerous and possibly malicious. They combat it with threats. However, with time, most SIXES gain some humor and insight into their own foibles to balance this "uptightness."

Strength and beauty in their partners and surroundings capture the attention of many SIXES. The other person in a SIX's life matters deeply. SIXES can be very committed and self- sacrificing, even while they find it difficult to believe in another person's love for them. Counting on someone else's love seems too painfully close to their original hurt.

Revising the SIX Strategy

SIXES need to examine their fears carefully to discriminate the imaginary from those with a factual basis. They seek help when they finally recognize that they have failed to attain what they wanted and have left many tasks incomplete. They have changed jobs, had trouble trusting bosses and co-workers, and often found reasons to back out when their projects were nearing successful completion.

The counter-phobic SIXES, who fought back in anger, need to know and appreciate the life-saving aspects of their early anger while recognizing that they now have other options. Most SIXES must also learn how to recognize and use their anger. For example, Ben admitted that he was anxious after an incident with a man who had shoved him on a streetcar the previous day:

> I told him, "Hey, watch it!" and he didn't do anything else. I don't know why I'm still upset.
> Therapist: But didn't you want to fight the man who shoved you?
> Ben: I would like to have shoved him out the door, but I didn't...I wouldn't...
> Therapist: What would you like to say that you didn't?
> Ben: Well, I'd like...
> Therapist: Say it to him.
> Ben: **Fuck off! I'm not going to let you dump your shit on me!**
> Therapist (handing him a canvas pillow): You would like to have hit him?
> Ben: No...not really.
> Therapist: Shove him out the door?
> Ben: Not really.
> Therapist: Imagine hitting him. Say out loud what comes into your mind.
> Ben: I'm really afraid...I'm really afraid.
> Therapist: What are you afraid might happen?
> Ben (in a smothered voice): I'm afraid, if I start, I won't stop hitting you. I'm afraid there is something wrong with me. I'm just as angry as you are. (Turning to therapist) I don't know what to do. I want to stop.
> Therapist: You don't want even to imagine your rage?
> Ben: Yeah.
> Therapist: You say you don't know what to do with your anger, and you refuse to imagine what to do.

Ben: I don't feel like it. It's stupid.
Therapist: So?
(Ben explodes, yells, hits pillows, shoves them out of the room)
Therapist: How do you feel?
Ben (breathing deeply): Satisfied...surprised. I didn't know I felt so strongly.

In this example from psychodrama, the therapist is not encouraging Ben to use real-life violence. Ben is finding how he uses his fear of his own rage to avoid knowing his appropriate anger. Later, going back to an earlier scene in his life where he felt the same way, he has to confront his highly abusive father, express the anger that he could not voice as a child and redecide that he can let himself know and use all his feelings. He now has to practice using all his feelings appropriately in the day-by-day interactions of his life.

The SIX's basic psychological task is to separate from the collective (group values) and sense one's separate reality in a solid way. Entering into the storm and stress of action makes this possible. Any exercise that shifts attention from the head to bodily feeling and action helps.

In therapy, as SIXES begin to overcome some of their fears, they often become suspicious of help and want to go it alone. Their fear of success, of becoming their own authority, becomes stronger for a time. It partly expresses a fear of outdoing their parents. They tend to focus on negative details and project their self-doubt so they think that others are doubtful of their abilities. They need help to recognize and celebrate their skills, their abilities and their successes.

This is a time when it is particularly important to have an ally. An example follows from a letter written to the author by Ivy Diton, who teaches emotionally disturbed children in Queens, New York. She describes change in a 14-year-old black girl living in a low-income housing project:

> Carrie is a giant, six feet tall. She weighs 145 pounds and looks masculine. I knew her from last year and dreaded having her in my homeroom class because I thought of her as a lunatic. She talked to herself, openly defied everyone, and bragged that other schools had kicked her out for hitting and throwing chairs at teachers.
>
> Nevertheless, as I got to know her, I realized she was both bright and sensitive. I listened as she told me one horrible story after another. She would come in before class began to tell me

about some atrocity that had happened in her neighborhood, then test me with some insane bit of behavior, laugh, scream or dance out of the room. I felt she wanted to be close to me but closeness frightened her.

We talked about everything, her personal grooming, life in a ghetto, being afraid of living sometimes. Her "crazy" behavior lessened. Her self-hatred began to move politically to her race, and in a class discussion about affirmative action, she challenged my more liberal views about blacks and told me that they were "all good-for-nothing druggies and would kill for some money to get drugs. No one wants to work or do anything." She cited her cousin, who was born to an aunt who didn't want him. He was subsequently raised by another aunt, then a grandmother, and now "he is in jail for the third time for drugs and stealing. He had so many chances and he kept messing up." As she spoke, anger and hopelessness were written all over her body.

I thought about the birth of my nephew and all the preparations, the nursery, the Lamaze classes, the emotional and financial preparation. It dawned on me to share this with Carrie. I asked her if this baby and her cousin had the same opportunities. She didn't say anything for several minutes as she thought—then she hugged me.

We continue to discuss issues. I've bought her *The Autobiography of Malcolm X*. I know I'm a role model for her. She has begun to develop friendships with other students.

Carrie's political-economic environment, which includes 70 percent unemployment, systematically conditions its participants to develop ego-states dominated by fear and doubt. In the ghettoes of America's cities, where black adolescents are under high stress, the major cause of death is teenage homicide.[3] Suicide is also frequent. Violent forms of mental illness and delinquency (the counter-phobic aggressive behavior of the SIX Program) are statistically high. The uncounted, less noticeable number of children suffering from depression is also significantly higher than in other sections of the country.

The work of healing societal pathology has to start with a better flow of information. Awareness of the conditioning processes can direct us to system-wide actions. Ivy Diton's care and attention allowed Carrie to find a base for her own self-esteem, but Carrie still has to face the continuing trauma of living in the system.

In alchemical symbolism, the tasks of the SIX strategy correspond in many ways to the *Mortificatio* state. Many sensitive people have a great reluctance to commit themselves to the individuation process, for they sense in advance the suffering that awaits them.

The high alertness of the SIX strategy to matters above and below ordinary consciousness allows access to a range of information not usually available to our materialistic and technological society. When SIXES master their fear, they have invaluable information to share and teach.

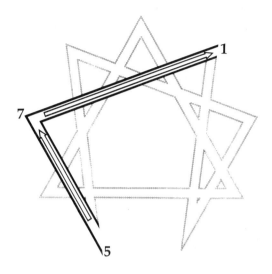

Point Seven: The Program of Easy Optimism with Uneasy Activity

Self-Definition: "I'm fun. I see the bright side of life."
Shadow Issue: Gluttony
Rejected Element: Pain
Addiction: Easy Optimism
Strength Needed: Level-headed moderation
Defense Mechanism: Rationalization
Psychological Disturbance: Narcissistic personality
Preoccupations Include: Maintaining high levels of stimulation, many activities, many things to do, wanting to stay "high."

Replacing deep contact with pleasant talking, planning, intellectualizing.

Defusing threat; maintaining a smokescreen of activity.

Charm as a first line of defense against fear. Talking one's way out of trouble.

Interrelating and systematizing information such that commitments necessarily include loopholes and other backup options which can lead to rationalized escape from difficult commitments, but can also lead to an ability to synthesize unusual connections and parallels between what appear to be antagonistic points of view.

Superiority/inferiority dichotomy.

Focus: Personal emphasis on savoring life.

Couple emphasis on being with people of like-mind.

Community emphasis on limits and obligations.

Life Task: To work with a sense of proportion and balance anchored in the now. Pain of any kind can serve as a steadying point of focus.

Even as THREES mirror economic success values, SEVENS reflect the social style of contemporary America.

The folly of easy optimism is similar to that of pessimism, in denying the wholeness of life. SEVENS avoid physical or psychological pain. Those who choose a SEVEN strategy plan their lives so that they are busy every second. They schedule a multitude of activities, moving at such a fast pace that there is no time for dealing with unpleasant events, or even for thinking about what they've done.

List-makers who don't want to take just one thing and develop it, SEVENS find it hard to choose priorities. Multi-track interests avoid boredom, limitation and emptiness, but above all allow SEVENS to avoid being pinned down.

> Jerry, a filmmaker, started his first film with a classmate's idea. Far more social than his friend, he made contacts with financial backers to put the film into production. This involved many meetings, trips to New York, lines of credit to establish. The friend, who had been his co-director, suddenly found himself an associate with only the promise of film credits. '
>
> Jerry, who also had considerable talent as a writer, was developing the film along lines the producers felt would make money. "Ducking, bobbing and weaving," he thoroughly enjoyed "playing with the big boys." Betrayal never entered his mind.

Parent-Child Issues

The SEVEN child had reason to fear in early childhood and developed a strategy of diffusion to deal with it. The child may have had a parent who modeled SEVEN behavior, or may have developed a slippery style of justifying his different interests in the face of threat. The parental messages he took in included:

"Don't grow up."

"Amuse me, or..." (Sheherazade)

"Don't be you."

(Optional:) "Don't be sane. Hurry up."

The SEVEN Program diverts attention away from potentially negative confrontations to more interesting imaginative alternatives.

The choice of a SEVEN strategy has three elements. First, it is difficult to hit a moving target, so the SEVEN avoids threat. Second, a multitude of interests guarantees that no one thing or person will ever be of such importance that its loss would be devastating. Third, the interests themselves are sufficiently absorbing that no energy is left over to consider less manageable matters.

SEVENS are often charmers and sometimes con artists. Their imaginations are positive in nature. People and situations that are overly serious, work-ridden or conflicted make them uncomfortable. Life should be fun, or at least interesting, and they know how to plan to make it happen. They see the value of what people tell them, but if it doesn't fit their experience, they figure it is only a point of view. They avoid dealing with unpleasant realities by mentally shifting into another place.

SEVENS flee from unpleasant confrontation, even when they suspect it could bring growth. They emphasize themselves, not their accomplishments, and not society. They neither judge others nor follow them. Going to the top of the scale in their profession doesn't interest them any more than anything else. Their goals are to be happy and not to miss anything. It is not easy for others to recognize that SEVENS are driven by fear, for they are great diverters. Anger is a true sign of intimacy; the person they get angry with matters to them.

SEVENS look for self-sufficiency in their partners, but they are not known for long-term commitments. They want an interesting sense of adventure with their friends, without anyone becoming too dependent or emotional. They want no contracts, only mutual agreements. The beginning of intimacy is sweet and enthusiastic, the middle is grounded in joint activities, but the end is a collapse.

> Stu met Kore in the student political movement of the early 70's. A sultry, exotic woman and passionate feminist, Kore also had formidable intellectual interests. Stu was drawn to her and awed and flattered by her response to him. They made a remarkable and effective team, an integral part of their community of friends. With the end of graduate school and entrance into their professions, Stu found the fun going out of "causes." He began to chafe at Kore's periodic, pessimistic self-doubt, blaming her for "putting herself in a mood." There weren't fights as such except those initiated by Kore's confrontations, but there were longer absences, more separate interests. Finally, he left: "Look, there's nothing going on between us. It doesn't make sense any longer."

The Enneagram SEVEN strategy deals with fear by fleeing into multiple activities which in turn prevent commitment and possible pain. This mindset is widely prevalent in relationship issues between contemporary men and women. In commitment to a person the rules can change. SEVENS fear the unpredictability of that. To make a commitment to a relationship means willingness to grapple together with whatever comes and to respond to each other authentically with spontaneous, instinctual truth. Fear of commitment is often awash with irrational fantasies, such as likening it to jail or a hospital where one's will and freedom are absent. Commitments are not to be taken lightly, but insofar as they come from free choice and will, they are an essential expression of the human spirit.

SEVENS do not see other people accurately because their own concerns absorb their attention. They want to share what they know, particularly that there is no one way of looking at things—but their observations tend to be vague. They have difficulty discriminating and knowing what is so.

They look for what is interesting and stimulating and are impatient with the mundane. They show people options, see what needs to be done and do it. They are more efficient when they have several things going on. They are addictive, finding it hard to stop doing whatever gives them pleasure, and they find a variety of ways to amuse themselves. If some is good, more is better.

For SEVENS, making plans takes precedence over present problems, which they tend to shirk. They put off difficult tasks. Once absorbed by a project, however, their enthusiasm mounts, and they work hard as long as the tasks go well. They prefer to work in spurts, however. Their procrastination and lack of punctuality may cause others to view them as unreliable.

SEVENS possess one invaluable trait, the ability to bring out playfulness in almost any family or group. They enjoy talk and entertaining gossip. They smile and laugh often, and find almost anyone easy to like.

Values held by SEVENS are widespread among today's affluent upper middle class. These values easily move this type of person from radical subjectivity and respect for the unique in each individual to a primary focus on self-stimulation and narcissism. We see examples of this in the market for "recreational" drugs, expensive health machines, sports equipment and electronic gadgets. SEVENS can create an idealized self-image, entitled to what they want and intolerant of criticism.

SEVENS use denial and rationalization as defense mechanisms; their mental disturbance takes the form of narcissism. Theodore Millon, in *Disorders of Personality*, describes narcissists as suffering few conflicts, inclined to trust others, and feeling confident that matters will work out well for them. They experience routine demands of ordinary life as annoying, demeaning incursions.

> They intrude upon the narcissist's cherished illusion of self as almost Godlike. Alibis to avoid 'pedestrian' tasks are easily mustered since narcissists are convinced that what they believe must be true and what they wish must be right.[4]

On the global scale, nations often behave in ways that might be considered infected with malignant narcissism, particularly when their actions prevent effective peacekeeping. Examples include the United States or the Soviet Union working to destabilize and overthrow the "unacceptable" elected governments of other countries; or nations like Brazil refusing to moderate the destruction of the rain forests despite their critical importance to the planet; or nations like Israel or South Africa denying civil rights to people whose rights to the land precede the existence of the state.

The focal concerns of SEVENS serve to maintain idealized images of life. Partnership SEVENS, for example, seek the security of belonging to a group of people who think the same way and mirror their own beliefs—e.g., a group of musicians in the same lifestyle or a likeminded political group. Communal SEVENS accept the limitations imposed by taking on obligations, albeit with a tinge of the martyr role, and look to the future for fulfillment. Personal SEVENS focus on heightening new experiences and ideas by positive imagination, savoring possibilities in advance. Fascination is the name of the game. M.F.K. Fisher's descriptions of meals in her cooking journals give the flavor of this style.

Revising the SEVEN Strategy

To live a levelheaded, moderate life is not initially an appealing goal to a SEVEN. As with any addict, the person has to reach bottom to realize that, under the glitter, his life lacks significant meaning. SEVENS usually become interested in working on themselves at midlife, when the difference between their actual situations and what they imagined their life would be becomes critical.

The alchemical term *Sublimatio* derives from a Latin word meaning "high" or "uplifted." It is an apt term for the SEVEN'S psychological strategy of dealing with a concrete problem by getting "above" it. The higher the SEVEN goes, the grander and more comprehensive the perspective but also the more remote and less likely to have a concrete effect.

SEVENS can develop a spiritual discipline but have difficulty separating insights from distractions. Rather than solve a problem, they put it off, forget about it or go off into imagining different ways of looking at it.

SEVENS progress in self-observation only when they can deal with their Shadow problem of greed for new experiences and possessions. One of the things SEVENS have to deal with is their unmet hunger for love. The need to belong is sometimes confused with the desire for possessions. Pain can awaken consciousness by forcing attention to one thing. SEVENS must stay with painful issues long enough to realize there is a problem. When fear arises, it can feel overwhelming and they must become aware of their evasions in dealing with it.

Their escapes are subtle variations of their Shadow traits. They shift attention to other matters, over-schedule themselves, take on several projects at a time, and "escape into health" as soon as the initial problem feels better. They become bored and want to quit when negative feelings need to be expressed. They feel stuck with their commitment to work on this and have problems with authority. They express anger by ridiculing the problem. By such signs we know something that isn't fun for them is happening. Progress is being made, and resisted, and the work continues.

The whole history of cultural evolution can be seen as a process in which human beings learn to see themselves and their world objectively, but it also carries an increasing danger of dissociation. Our complex society, with its multiple levels of incessant information, demands constant attention, decisions and action. When the SEVEN strategy matures to include the dark side of life, it models an integration of opposites suited to survive this period in history.

Summary of the Anxiety and Flight Response Group

The FIVE child decides that people threaten something essential to her survival. She develops a protective strategy of playing possum, camouflaging her existence and reducing her needs to a minimum so that she becomes as unnoticeable as possible. She then discovers that she can pursue her own interests undisturbed.

SIXES' strategy is to focus on danger, to scan the environment for all possible threats and to program their behavior to avoid them. An alternative, if they can muster the strength, is to meet danger head on and defuse it.

The choice of a SEVEN strategy has three elements. First, it is difficult to hit a moving target, so the SEVEN avoids threat. Second, a multitude of interests guarantees that no one thing or person will ever be of such importance that its loss would be devastating. Third, the interests themselves are sufficiently absorbing that no energy is left over to consider less manageable matters.

FIVE

Life Script Program: Knowledge with withdrawal
Self-definition/self-image: "I'm perceptive."
Shadow issue: Miserliness
Rejected transformation element: Meaninglessness
Addiction: Knowledge
Virtue/strength needed: Detachment
Defense mechanism: Isolation (compartmentalization)
Psychological disturbance: Avoidant personality

SIX

Life Script Program: Security with fear and doubt
Self-definition/self-image: "I'm loyal. I'm cautious."
Shadow issue: Cowardice or counter-phobic reckless courage
Rejected transformation element: Originality
Addiction: Security
Virtue/strength needed: Courage (Faith)
Defense mechanism: Projection
Psychological disturbance: Anxiety disorder, paranoid schizophrenia

SEVEN

Life Script Program: Easy Optimism with Uneasy Activity
Self-definition/self-image: "I'm fun. I see the bright side of life."
Shadow issue: Gluttony
Rejected transformation element: Pain
Addiction: Easy Optimism
Virtue/strength needed: Level-headed moderation
Defense mechanism: Rationalization
Psychological disturbance: Narcissistic personality

Chapter Three:

The Programs of Anger and Fight

The Program of Self-defined Justice with Arrogance
The Program of Non-aggression with Indolence and Indecision
The Program of Perfection With Resentment

Photo by Stanton Nelson

Eyes narrow, attention focuses closely on the other, blood pressure rises, lips curl, sounds form in the throat, the body prepares for action and possible violence. In the animal world, territorial conflicts, defense of offspring and competition for a mate trigger the fight response for survival and dominance.

Anger provides the focus to identify the source of trouble and the energy to change it.

Our physiology is mammalian, but humans have complex ways of experiencing anger which our language reflects—resentment, irritation, annoyance, exasperation, indignation, wrath, rage, fury, animosity, vindictiveness, sullenness, petulance, irascibility, bitterness and malevolence, among others. We fear anger when it is out of control in rage and mob violence, but each Enneagram point has its own connection to one of the programs governed by anger. We either express it, deny it and avoid conflict, or simmer with resentment, neither expressing it nor letting it go.

Anger is an essential emotion, closely connected to our capacity for survival, choice and freedom. The path for release from anger entails knowledge of how to use it effectively to change what is intolerable.

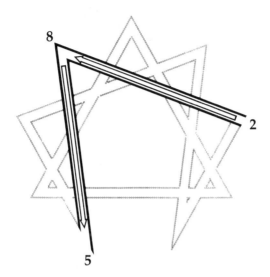

Point Eight: The Program of Self-defined Justice with Arrogance

Self-Definition: "I can do. I'm powerful."
Shadow Issue: Lust — use of others as objects
Rejected Element: Weakness
Addiction: Arrogant justice
Strength Needed: Trust
Defense Mechanism: Denial
Psychological Disturbance: Sociopath
Preoccupations Include: Aggression and impulse control.
Puritan/hedonist dichotomy.

Control of personal objects, space and people likely to influence the EIGHT'S life.

Excessive (to others) self-presentation—too much, too loud.

Tendency to see things in extremes, people either strong or weak, fair or unfair, with no middle ground; an automatic denial of other points of view in favor of single "legitimate" opinion that supports the EIGHT'S security.

Concern with justice and the protection of others.

Focus: Personal emphasis on satisfactory survival.

Couple emphasis on possession/surrender.

Community emphasis on friendship.

Life Task: Realization of truth and justice in each moment's flow of reality. Accepting one's personal weakness offers the possibility of integration.

EIGHTS function well as prosecuting attorneys, corporate chief executives, Mafia bosses, and sometimes even as therapeutic and spiritual gurus. Friedrich Nietzsche, Pablo Picasso, Gurdjieff and Saul Alinsky are well-known exemplars, but the personality is also found among juvenile delinquents and sociopaths. Their favorite defense mechanism is denial. They want the focus outside and on the action.

Fritz Perls, founder of gestalt therapy, and Chuck Dederich, originator of Synanon, a community treatment for drug addiction, were EIGHTS who developed powerful methods of awareness training and behavior change. All EIGHTS seem to have some essential gift and issue centering in the instinctual use of power.

Parent-Child Issues

For this Program, whatever messages the parent sends are important only insofar as the child develops skills to fight them. Children with an EIGHT strategy hear the messages:

"Don't be you."

"Don't feel what you feel."

Anger is often used by these children to defend themselves against "nice," smothering parents. They preserve their right to think and feel, thereby avoiding the banality of what they sense is an insipid life.

Children who feel unfairly controlled and limited by the people who surround them may learn to control their anxiety and the feelings of others by experimenting with anger. Such children learn to imitate what they perceive as parental intimidation. Their primary interest is to attain a sense of personal security.

The EIGHT strategy is to seize control and emotional dominance. The child decides to define the game rather than be defined by it. Feeling the power to do this, the child denies her or his own vulnerability.

As these children grow, they avoid any show of personal weakness. They view life as a power struggle between topdogs and underdogs, and they intend to stay on top. They use intimidation and often seem to be looking for a fight. They say "No!" to others easily and have no remorse in putting people down. EIGHTS have no intention of letting others take advantage of them. They are always ready for confrontation. They enjoy unmasking pretense and injustice and using expressive, vulgar language. They sense others' weaknesses and are ready to attack should they be provoked.

The Synanon Game, which developed from Chuck Dederich's personal style of interaction, can perhaps give a sense of the EIGHT process. John Enright, saying "It's clearly not a 'Let's sit down and talk about this' of therapy," comes closest to capturing its qualities.[1] A feature of the game is the indictment, some piece of behavior or action which is brought into the game and examined. The group confronts a person with his behavior. Perhaps he was ten minutes late for an appointment or was rough-tempered in some out-of-game setting.

The behavior can be large or small, important or trivial. The one making the indictment delivers it in a scathing, righteous manner with outrageously exaggerated details. Immediately, others join in with similar incidents they have observed and everyone begins to weave a net around the indicted person to establish his thoroughly irresponsible attitudes, habits and character. Whenever he attempts to justify or defend himself, the group attacks his style of defense itself.

The goal is to strip away every mask, expose every evasion, to drive the person out of his usual ways of hiding and not taking responsibility. A good game has high comedy. Players of the game can reduce the epic to a gag, a momentary lapse of awareness into a monumental defect. Anyone with word skills can seize leadership, which bounces from person to person. Everyone, even the most shy, learns the skill sooner or later, usually by attacking someone who is a mirror image of himself. In the game people work through their disagreements, express their negative feelings, carry out their quarrels and dominance struggles, let off steam and begin to explore and express new, more powerful parts of themselves. For many people, the game is helpful, but only when it is contained in the context of a caring community.[2]

EIGHTS feel challenged to pull down all those who assert power or who see themselves as superior. They feel most alive when they are in control. They enjoy being strong and respect others who are strong, quickly losing respect for anyone who seems to compromise on issues. Unless they are met with firmness, they tend to bulldoze others. They have difficulty admitting, much less expressing, their softer, more tender feelings.

EIGHTS think people create their own problems by being gullible, weak and halfhearted. EIGHTS are quite willing to shape them up. They push for what they see as right and are willing to take on the whole power structure, if necessary, to gain their points. Their strength is strong love, and in their self-assertion they model ways by which others can express their real feelings.

The ability of EIGHTS to get attention focused on their issues can serve the needs of the group. EIGHTS do not hide their dissatisfactions. They bring them out where they can be dealt with. As children, their vandalism was often motivated by revenge or by their feelings for the helpless underdog. Other children could manipulate and use them because they would take risks when they thought some injustice had been done.

They feel a need to control their own environment, a need to be directors and eliminate surprises. EIGHTS always know who and what they are dealing with. They enjoy provoking people in order to find out more about them, especially their malevolent behavior. "I want to know their weaknesses so I know where to get them if I need to."

For an EIGHT, anger brings out the truth. Eye contact is important, and they use it to determine feelings. They don't like weakness, which feels like manipulation to make them the aggressor. Anger is their feeling of choice. They are comfortable with others' anger, if it is open. They cannot tolerate hidden messages or indirectness. EIGHTS narrow attention to questions of personal security, and this reflects in their focal preoccupations.

Their partnership style emphasizes possession and surrender in one-to-one couple relationships. The relationship has to be so trustworthy that control can be completely given over. The communal EIGHT carries a version of this into friendship, extending trust to those he protects and who protect him. The survival focus translates these concerns into the mechanics and management of personal space to maintain satisfactory survival.

EIGHTS do not necessarily allow their feelings for justice to stand in the way of their self-interest. King David of the Old Testament was an EIGHT. One day the prophet Nathan came to David and told him a story:

> There were two men, one rich and the other poor. The rich man had many flocks and herds, but the poor man had only one little ewe lamb, which he had bought. And it grew up with him and his children. It used to eat from his morsel and drink from his cup and was like a daughter to him. One day a traveler came to the rich man, who was unwilling to take from his flocks to prepare a feast. Instead he took the poor man's lamb and used it for the meal.

David's sense of justice was outraged:

> As the Lord lives, the man who has done this deserves to die. He shall restore the lamb fourfold, for he has no pity.

Nathan said to David:

> You are the man.[3]

The story deals with David's falling in love with Bathsheba, the wife of one of his generals. He arranged for Uriah, the husband, to be sent to the front where he would be killed. Then David could marry Bathsheba.

Peter Berger, a sociologist of religion, describes this story as full of deceptions, most of them perpetrated by David on himself to supply alibis for his actions. First, his rationalizations: It was not his fault he had come into the world with such lustful loins (libido). This led to the second deception, that it was not murder but the logic of war orders that led Uriah to die in battle—*c'est la guerre*. The third deception: As an Oriental king, he had this prerogative.

His true conscience, in the person of Nathan, cut through these layers of deceptions and excuses in a single stroke.[4]

Revising the EIGHT Strategy

When EIGHTS recognize their intolerance for feelings of vulnerability, they can begin to admit a wider range of emotional qualities—and start moving from a dominator relationship model to partnership.

In the Synanon organization, when Chuck Dederich married, a new type of game emerged in which the target person was bombarded with appreciation. For several years, until Betty Dederich died and Chuck regressed in grief, their fruitful union encouraged new forms of growth and creativity.

The Shadow issue of the EIGHT strategy is lust or desirousness. Edward Edinger, in *Anatomy of the Psyche,* calls it "the coagulated aspect of psyche."[5] The alchemical term associated with the EIGHT'S process is *Coagulatio*. The lure of desire links the sweetness of fulfillment with the forbidden. As in the story of Adam and Eve, its attainment brings guilt and punishment—but also self-will and consciousness. The theme is found in various tales and myths throughout the centuries. One must descend before finding the way through. One must become conscious of one's own evil, one's Shadow qualities, to contribute to the real world.

EIGHTS rarely enter therapy because they fear that the therapist will control them (their old issue from childhood). But their depression, substance abuse and assaultive behavior can cause family members to persuade them into treatment. They need a therapist who is consistent in expectations, someone whom they can learn to trust by fighting, someone who will meet them on their own ground and not back away when their wounded feelings and self-hatred emerge. EIGHTS need to notice how their behavior creates adversarial relationships and how they replace their moderate wishes with excessive stimulation. They need to know how others manipulate them. Insights have to be repeated many times to combat their pervasive denial and "forgetting." Any signs of vulnerability, dependency or compromise need to be supported.

EIGHTS bring zest to whatever they do: working, playing or meeting new challenges. They are ready to get involved and deliver intensity to any project. The mature EIGHT, who has accepted vulnerability as a fact of the human condition, acquires a compassionate strength to deal with almost anything.

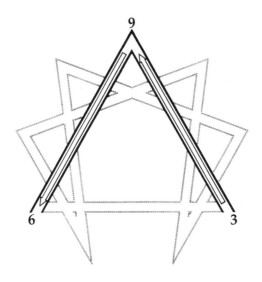

Point Nine: The Program of Non-aggression with Indolence and Indecision

Self-Definition: "I'm easy-going."
Shadow Issue: Laziness
Rejected Element: Conflict
Addiction: Indecision/Inaction
Strength Needed: Action (Love)
Defense Mechanism: Narcotization; "shutting off the juice"
Psychological Disturbance: Obsessive/passive aggressive personality
Preoccupations Include: Dichotomy of belief/doubt.
Dichotomy of mystical/worldly concerns.
Replacing essential needs with inessential substitutes.
Indecisiveness and difficulty saying "no".
Containment of physical energy and anger.
Control through stubbornness and passive aggression.
Fluctuating attitudes, oppositional behavior and emotions—either to adhere to the desires of others as a means of gaining security, or to be defiantly resistant and independent.
Difficulty in maintaining a personal point of view, but ability to recognize and support another's position.
Fight-phobic: avoiding conflict by not knowing the anger within.
Focus: Personal emphasis on appetite.
Couple emphasis on union.
Community emphasis on participation.
Life Task: To experience love guided by the strength of taking actions appropriate to any given situation, including conflict.

Throughout the contemporary world, large numbers of people experience themselves as invisible to those in power: for example, South African blacks, Southeast Asian and Central American refugees, black urban teenagers, and mothers living in poverty in the United States. Not to be seen or acknowledged is enraging. To the degree that we are social creatures and depend on others to define us, the external view is inexorably taken in: "I do not matter."

Parent-Child Issues

How does a child deal with parents who habitually overlook his/her wishes? The child who chooses a NINE strategy feels his/her parents are indifferent or lack affection. The parental messages convey:

"Don't."

"Don't bother me."

"Don't be (don't exist)."

Perhaps the mother has other priorities, or fears spoiling her children. NINES come to cope with such absence of love by saying that nothing in life matters much anyway. They seem to deny their own worth and importance, no matter what their later achievements. With impassive faces and monotonous voices, even with body language and dress, they appear to say, "I do not really matter."

> Eddy remembered his childhood as long afternoons in an empty house. His physician father and politician mother were each in active careers; his bright and social older brothers were away in boarding school. He had been instructed not to talk to the cook for fear of picking up her accent and poor grammar. Eddy had a photographic memory and could remember every detail of the house, even the wallpaper.

The child develops substitutes, excessive amounts of food or enormous amounts of information, to dilute anxiety and divert anger when adults overlook his needs.

The NINE personality could be characterized in the terms Gurdjieff uses, as self-forgetting to the neglect of self-observation.

NINES are asleep to personal motives. Their perception includes everything, but nothing stands out as more important than anything else. In their ambivalence between rebellion and conforming, NINES choose to withdraw. They experience life from a very low energy level and feel they need to avoid tension. They numb their own reactions and let their consciousness drift. They focus on personal memories or quirky details. They do not necessarily space out; they simply have a strong desire not to take a position or oppose anyone.

> Eddy, age six, with unrecognized eye problems, sat in the back of the room with other boys of his own height. Unable to see the blackboard, he learned to put himself into a trance, watching the slow movement of the classroom clock. Three years later, teachers discovered his eye defects. "Why didn't you say something?" they asked. He looked at them blankly. Two years later, they discovered his 185 IQ. "Why didn't we notice?" they might have asked.

The NINE strategy arises from the self-perception of not being important enough to love. The child turns this inward. Nothing (and no one) is more important than anything (or anyone) else.

Although aware of the complexity in an event, NINES find it difficult to select and express the important facts. When confronted, they believe they have to buy time. Layers of defense are present between "self" and the "other person." An inner rehearsal goes on before they can respond.

When they become anxious in conversation, they diffuse their attention, either into rumination about some bit of problem solving, or outward, toward details in the environment. One NINE compared his style of attention to a radio drifting from station to station, picking up different frequencies. NINES find it hard to stay focused and describe their consciousness as rather like a dream state.

NINES sense what is essential for their partners and desire to be in harmony with them. When conflicts occur, NINES deny the importance of the issues causing the conflicts. They discriminate poorly between the essential and the peripheral and, as a result, may undertake much activity with little value or purpose.

> Eddy easily completed the assigned sets of math problems and spent his time playing solitaire—"three years, three hundred thousand games."

NINES can become TV "couch potatoes," addicted to their regular shows, enjoying a static familiar life and generally avoiding going out to new experiences of any kind. Because they avoid becoming excited about anything, they often put off doing things, are often late for appointments, and sometimes forget them entirely. Time seems to pass by, and they do not know where it goes. Although they find it difficult to make decisions, when they do form an opinion they hang onto it quite firmly.

Those who choose a NINE strategy pick up the larger picture and develop an ability to see all sides of an issue. Their peacefulness influences the people around them. NINES listen without making negative judgments about anything confided to them. They rarely give much advice, but can help others put their problems in perspective. They are natural mediators and useful in settling conflict. One friend described a NINE: "He's never an adversary, always an advocate."

However, personal desires and expectations can feel dangerous. They do not trust their own, often considerable, abilities. They forget what is important to themselves. The more crucial a thing is, the easier to blank out. They constantly avoid what they are supposed to do. Compliments are difficult for them to accept. They do not like surprises. They want to control as much of their lives as possible. They prefer to stay hidden because what others might expect of them is unclear. They may try to do everything and so lose what is essential.

As children, NINES made an early decision to go along with what others needed or wanted in order to hold what little love was available. When NINES find and express their anger at this discounting, they also find a more spontaneous self. Because of their difficulty in determining personal positions, they tend to mirror and identify with the inner condition of all types. They identify with such preoccupations as a personal survival focus anchoring in appetite, the passion to lose themselves in union with a beloved other as their couple focus; and the communal instinct expressed in belonging to groups involved with social causes or special activities.

The Enneagram NINE strategy for dealing with threat is not to submit, flee—or fight. NINES avoid anger by keeping the anger buried. Their favorite defense mechanism is narcotization. Others experience them as "shutting off the juice." When they use drugs to do this, there is a close parallel to some societal addictions. Addicts abuse substances or processes to maintain or increase the state of unconsciousness. They divert their attention and limit their awareness of disturbances and pain that might otherwise force change.

Some societal addictions are obvious and function in the same way to limit awareness of social disturbances and pain. The pervasive use of television absorbs vast amounts of available time and consciousness, limits connection with other sources of information, and discourages active thought and judgment. Sophisticated commercial messages encourage a state of desire, narrowing and focusing consciousness on consumption without consideration of the costs and world consequences. This fragmentation of consciousness poses an almost insurmountable obstacle to forming a coherent sense of genuine community life.

Revising the NINE Strategy

The NINE enters therapy sometimes after substance abuse or failures to follow out commitments. Depression, passive aggression and finally rage surface when non-essential activities halt. Successful intervention is best done with a change of environment and behavior modification techniques of reward reinforcement. Support for a new habit should be unconditional. Anger provides the energy to change and needs to be brought out. Every number has to be called what it is: "blaming," "withholding," "going stubborn." NINES have an idea that simple tasks are overwhelming. They are sensitive to having their efforts overlooked, criticized or discounted, so they need to receive full credit. They tend to consider plans to complete a project equivalent to having it done, so they need to be questioned about their follow-through.

Their Shadow problem of indolence is almost impervious to the ordinary forms of motivation through discomfort and hope. More than any other type, they need the active support and challenge of another person, or other people who unquestionably care for them and who are willing to give them time and interest.

Waking up as individuals is essential to the transformation of collective consciousness. The slow, painstaking work of responsible engagement with our individual lives, neighborhood and country requires understanding the resources we have in each other and the network of our relationships. The NINE insight that everything and everyone are connected aids this awareness.

The alchemical analogy of *Coniunctio* is symbolically linked to the NINE position in the Enneagram as a goal in the great union of opposites. Change, however, can only come from within and after a long, difficult and dangerous journey of transformation. The mature NINE strategy flows from awareness of the connections of all reality and moves with detached caring and compassion to do whatever is necessary in whatever society it finds itself. Love is an objective virtue, not a passion. It grows stronger with practice.

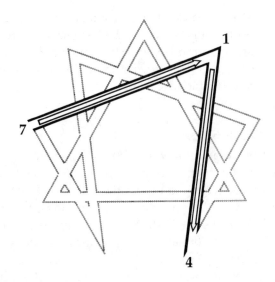

Point One: The Program of Perfection with Resentment

Self-Definition: "I'm right. I'm hard-working."
Shadow Issue: Wrath
Rejected Element: Direct expression of anger
Addiction: Perfection
Strength Needed: Forbearance, serenity
Defense Mechanism: Reaction formation
Psychological Disturbance: Compulsive personality
Preoccupations Include: Demanding internal standards.

Difficulty acknowledging personal desires that conflict with these standards of correctness.

Comparing self to others and concern about criticism.

Compulsive worry about wrong decisions.

Self-righteous displacement of anger towards what appear to be legitimate outside targets.

Focus on error (which can develop superb powers of criticism, including humor).

Conflict between rigidity and sensitivity.

Focus: Personal emphasis on worry.

Couple emphasis on jealousy.

Community emphasis on consistency and firmness.

Life Task: To achieve a sense of serenity with a body secure in its capacities. As projections are worked through and resentment has been tamed, compassion becomes possible.

Anger is a tricky emotion. Contemporary psychologists can say what they will about its importance as protest and as a way of locating what needs changing in our lives, but balancing the expression of anger against the requirements of family and social life is complex. For centuries, our culture has emphasized control of anger. Abuse of children outrages us, urban violence frightens us, but the power of anger continues to fascinate us.

Perfectionists appear to be our point men. They experiment with a strategy to acquire the power of anger, then control its expression through internalized rules. The cost is high. Rules preoccupy them. They judge and monitor their own behavior according to the rules, constantly compare themselves to others, and think about all issues in terms of right or wrong.

> Burt: "I resent bad drivers, the guys who pass on curves, who don't signal lane changes and that sort of thing. It feels good to let out some of my anger with my horn, giving them the finger."
>
> Jane: "My internal standards are so high that I can't meet them and, of course, no one else can either. My judgments run a constant undercomment with any man I date. I don't lose the relationship, just the sense of pleasure."
>
> Lenny: "I'm my own worst critic—'that was bad,' 'I shouldn't have said that.' It's like acid inside. If something I've done isn't absolutely right, it's wrong, no shades of gray."

Perfectionists dissemble their strong desire to assert themselves, act independently and defy the regulations, but resentment betrays them. They can't swallow it and they won't spit it out. They hold it between clenched teeth.

Parent-Child Issues

The resentment originally comes from the burden of other people's expectations. The task of figuring out what the power people want begins in childhood, when the child feels severely criticized and inadequate to the demands placed on him or her. It is as if the child were constantly instructed:

"Don't be a child."

"Work hard."

"Be perfect."

> When Lenny's mother became impatient with his slow response to toilet training, she forced him to conform to a schedule. He initially responded to her with rage and defiance,

but when she backed up her rules with threats and punishment, he began to obey.

The rules extended to other matters. Whenever he failed to obey, his parents made him feel guilty and ask forgiveness. He learned to cover his rage. Eventually what he himself wanted was forgotten and replaced by the rules, what others viewed as good. He had introjected (taken in as part of himself) his demanding, perfectionist and condemning parents.

By adolescence, Lenny had fully incorporated the regulations. His merciless internal conscience evaluated and controlled all his behavior, making him doubt and hesitate before he acted. He had great difficulty turning in school assignments before the deadline. His thoughts became mired in detail. He was indecisive, mistrustful and easily upset by the unfamiliar or deviations from his routines. Guilt and self-recrimination settled in, so he looked for more rules and drew the noose even tighter.

People who choose a perfectionist strategy are not usually so visibly disturbed. In fact, they form the core of most professions.

ONES' strategy, which they develop in childhood, is to find out the rules of the game and master them in order to do a good job, and thereby win approval if not love. They want to have a means of judging others and their place in relation to them.

Perfectionists can be socially charming and good conversationalists, for they notice everything. They are exceptionally orderly, punctual, systematic, methodical, industrious, consistent and meticulous. They embody all the social values of our American culture, including its ambivalent mistrust of anger. They make excellent judges, soldiers, engineers and surgeons. Their critical thinking can be challenging. Usually fair-minded and honest, they see through pretenses of superiority, but others often feel an undercurrent of discomfort when with them.

As they follow the Program, they develop an austere life, but it eliminates ambiguity and uncertainty. Their structure sustains their values. They hold dangerous feelings like defiance and anger in check, but something is askew. Since they are constantly concerned with perfection, nothing ever measures up. The attempt to be perfect absorbs endless amounts of energy, and they are always slightly depressed by being less than perfect.

ONES, having chosen the strategy of perfection, always seem dissatisfied about something. They avoid expressing anger directly and sometimes don't even recognize it. It shows, however, in the note of irritation in their voices, in the high-strung edginess of their behavior. Fuzziness in thought or action is unacceptable. They think others should realize their own faults and correct them without prompting. Their compulsive behavior, which others view as industrious and efficient, lacks spontaneity and flexibility. They want to know exactly what is going on and what they can count on.   They like predictability.

ONES are not always glum, but their serious-mindedness is striking. Posture and movement embody an underlying tightness and emotions kept well in check.

> Jenna teaches high school math, a job she dislikes. She took it on because she couldn't decide what else to do. She works hard and spends as much time as necessary to create lesson plans that are above criticism. She resents any disorder left by other teachers. Always cleaning up and putting things in order, she never fully relaxes. Small things take up all her time. Keeping track of so much detail prevents her from dealing with larger issues in her life, like finding out what she wants to do.

When frustrated and dissatisfied, a frequent state, ONES become impatient with the limitations of time and human nature. Although compulsive about detail analysis, if they can keep up with their demands on themselves, they are psychologically healthy. With lack of time or energy, however, they feel overwhelmed, become discouraged, and fall into depressed moodiness, accomplishing almost nothing. Internal tension sometimes causes psychosomatic difficulties.

Their inner anger, fueled by a "gunny sack" of current and past frustrations, seems inexhaustible.

> Burt: "I've a grudge list like a computer file. Every couple of years, I roll it out to people. I've been keeping a mental list of everything they're doing wrong."

ONES are prickly in close contact. They find it hard to admit that they hurt. They rarely permit anyone to see the emptiness they often feel behind their accomplishments. They respond to vulnerability in others, but find it hard to show their own or to ask for what they want. They interpret sympathy as condescension when they are in pain. Nonetheless, they yearn for love, and when another cares, they can and do respond.

In social situations, ONES tend to be polite and formal, relating to others in terms of rank and status. They seem deferential, ingratiating and even obsequious to those of higher rank. When dealing with subordinates, in their worst moments they are autocratic, condemnatory, pompous, self-righteous and rigidly insistent on rules.

Because of their ambivalence between conformity and defiance, and the imperative need to control their hostility, compulsive personalities use more varied defensive mechanisms than other ego types. Two of the most effective are identification and sublimation. Identification poses some problems. If ONES find a punitive model of authority to emulate, they can justify venting hostile impulses.

Their other defenses do not provide outlets for anger, but keep hostility in check. For example, in reaction formation (doing the opposite of one's impulse), ONES substitute kindness for cruelty. ONES find value both in isolation (separating the problem or person from the other facets of their life) and undoing (acting in ways that take back or deny an earlier action).

Sub-types refer to the dominant preoccupations and style of the personality. The couple sub-type becomes jealous when she compares herself to whatever or whomever the mate values. The personal survival sub-type worries about the collision of personal wishes with ideas of what is correct and a desire for perfection. The community sub-type does not adapt to anyone else's definition of his or her condition. For example:

> Burt, a 45-year-old engineer, was unable to hold a job for more than six months because of his uncompromising stance that he "would not play politics." Over and over again he found that his boss expected him to be a team player and support some professional compromise that he found intolerable. As pressure mounted, he vacillated between anxiety and explosive outbursts, which eventually would cost him his job.
>
> He came to therapy only when he had run out of money and his wife had insisted she would no longer carry the household expenses. He regarded therapy as an encroachment, but he agreed to try it for two reasons. First, he was uncomfortable being out of work for over a year. Second, he knew his wife was absorbed in her own therapeutic experience, and he was jealous of her interest in it.
>
> Only after weeks of testing the therapist's "objectivity" could he trust that she would not condemn him. He then began to see how his inner anger and resentment was structuring his life. As a child he had learned to take care of his parents by always being agreeable, but he felt alive inside only when he sensed the energy of his anger exploding. He channeled much of it into political

causes, but recently he seemed to feel a growing surplus which leaked into his work. He knew he was sarcastic and bored. One day, in a psychodrama role reversal, he admitted that others viewed him as stubborn, spiteful and vindictive.

Now, in working with this Shadow part of himself, he began to understand that he wanted to be in control of his situation, not labeled or locked in. As he started going directly toward what he wanted and as others responded by giving it to him, he realized his anxiety increased. This wasn't part of the script!

Revising the ONE Strategy

The first step is to find the suppressed anger in the day-by- day events of life. Sometimes angry children frighten themselves as they realize what violence they can generate, and from then on they suppress their anger. No matter what the provocation, ONES must recognize that they can choose not to act in a way hurtful to themselves or anyone else. However, they need to experience and express the feeling. Fantasies can serve to bring the anger into clearer focus.

Struggling with wrath is often symbolized by fire. Alchemical symbolism starts with *Calcinatio*, a fiery process to drive out impurities. To the extent that ONES succeed in enlarging and extending their ego consciousness in this struggle, they are less likely to be caught in emotional storms.

An important spiritual task for ONES is recognizing their ability to choose feelings, then moving toward freedom and pleasure. Next comes learning to acknowledge their own spontaneous impulses: not only anger but the unmet needs it covers. The rules have to be broken to allow ONES to express a deeper initiative and self-trust. ONES must move away from rigidity and concern with right behavior; they must learn detachment from an outcome. They must abandon their tendency to judge their own performances in terms of the highest standards. They must allow themselves to be "beginners" and "intermediates" in the skills they want to master.

ONES must allow the possibility that the game they defined does not exist, that the world is much more complex and multidimensional than they have imagined. They have to stop overscheduling themselves in order to allow both a wider awareness and a more playful self to emerge. Often deepening the pleasures of sexuality is a beginning of this awareness.

ONES, who feel they cannot exist without the structure of "knowing the way things should be," might take on the rule ascribed to Krishnamurti, "Don't compare." It is not an easy rule for the ONE to learn.

We must not underestimate the struggle with the Shadow issue of wrath. We enjoy anger ("Make my day!"). We easily cross the line between spontaneous anger and half-conscious cruelty. Wrath takes many forms and can feed itself with hate-filled relish. Cold rage stifles our discrimination and warm-heartedness.

Assumptions entangled with anger need to be challenged. Consciously, or unconsciously, ONES assume they need their anger in order to be powerful and effective. They use their anger to justify behavior they wouldn't otherwise permit. When their "gunny sack" is sufficiently filled with resentments, then they justify doing what they wish.

> Therapist: What's wrong with simply deciding you don't want the job? How come you have to be so angry to quit?
> ONE: It wouldn't make sense... You can't just quit without a good reason.
> Therapist: Who told you that? Sounds like part of the old program. (The client's use of the word "you" instead of "I" is a clue to an internalized parental message instead of a personal judgment.)

Sometimes nations behave like ONES, waiting for a last straw to justify the outbreak of major hostilities. In union-management negotiations, one side or the other looks for similar incidents before the walkout or lockout. At different periods in history, a ONE Program has dominated an entire society, for example, the New England Puritans.

Enormous pools of resentment lie waiting to be tapped. We need to examine the tide of irritability in our country, evident in the rising number of lawsuits. People need help in understanding and coping with their feelings. Mediation in family disputes, divorces and neighborhood conflicts is available in some communities. Use of legal arbitration and negotiators allow ONE-type communal angers to be met and contained.

The issue is to discriminate the valuable ONE qualities in specific situations. Engineers and surgeons, for example, need to cultivate the precision and care of the ONE Program.

The particular gift of the ONE orientation, a sense of awe and longing for the perfection of completion, the inclusion of everything in perfect harmony and balance, permits a very high level of spiritual awareness.

Summary of the Anger and Fight Response Group

The EIGHT strategy is to seize control and emotional dominance. The child decides to define the game rather than be defined by it. Feeling the power to do this, the child denies her or his own vulnerability.

The NINE strategy arises from the self-perception of not being important enough to love. The child turns this inward. Nothing (and no one) is more important than anything (or anyone) else.

ONES' strategy, which they develop in childhood, is to find out the rules of the game and master them in order to do a good job, and thereby win approval if not love. They want to have a means of judging others and their place in relation to them.

EIGHT

Life Script Program: Self-defined justice with arrogance
Self-definition/self-image: "I can do. I'm powerful."
Shadow issue: Lust — use of others as objects
Rejected transformation element: Weakness
Addiction: Arrogant justice
Virtue/strength needed: Trust
Defense mechanism: Denial
Psychological disturbance: Sociopath

NINE

Life Script Program: Non-aggression with indolence and indecision
Self-definition/self-image: "I'm easy-going."
Shadow issue: Laziness
Rejected transformation element: Conflict
Addiction: Indecision/Inaction
Virtue/strength needed: Action (Love)
Defense mechanism: Narcotization; "shutting off the juice"
Psychological disturbance: Obsessive/passive aggressive personality

ONE

Life Script Program: Perfection with resentment
Self-definition/self-image: "I'm right. I'm hard-working."
Shadow issue: Wrath
Rejected transformation element: Direct expression of anger
Addiction: Perfection
Virtue/strength needed: Forbearance, serenity
Defense mechanism: Reaction formation
Psychological disturbance: Compulsive personality

Epilogue to Part I

Before moving your attention to the means of change in Part II, you may want to examine how change happens within an Enneagram position, as well as the costs and consequences. You may want to test your own Enneagram position with the following exercise, which requires your using active imagination to respond to a series of questions.

Growth in consciousness comes through making choices in response to moral issues. The situation you'll consider requires such a decision. It deals with betrayal, one of the central experiences in human life. As you track your decisions in this exercise, you may identify the sector of the Enneagram in which you are working. You can compare the feelings, defenses and Shadow issues you find with the descriptions in Part I.

Think of a major betrayal in your own life, in the outer world, or in history. This is not necessarily the one you will work with, but the first one that comes to mind. Is it one in which your very survival seemed threatened? Or was it the tearing apart of closeness in relationship? Or perhaps the betrayal of a political cause? As you examine the type of betrayal, find your focal concern and your *instinctive, passionate response* to it. The way you experience your Enneagram issues is highly conditioned by this initial division—your survival, relationship or communal focus.

Now we'll move into this more deeply. Select a betrayal that you experienced: perhaps by a family member, a teacher, a friend or a lover.

Don't read any further until you have this problem clearly in mind.

Go back to the time when you first sensed that something might be wrong. What was your initial feeling response: fear, confusion, outrage, despair, jealousy? Remember that in a stressful situation, we initially use the defenses of our central Enneagram point to deal with it. Then, as the difficulties mount, we move into the defenses of our stress point, but also have access to the preceding point.

As the evidence of betrayal became clear, what did you do? Did you examine how you might be wrong, distorting or exaggerating what was happening, in order to explain it away? Did you fight, flee, or figure that there was nothing you could do about it anyway?

In the critical moments, when you are being torn apart by your own trustfulness, a dangerous choice appears. Consider the following to find the responses that you are inclined to make. These responses are not necessary but possible within the identified Enneagram Programs.

Revenge (EIGHT): EIGHTS tend to act on their anger. You fight evil with evil, an eye for an eye, a tooth for a tooth. If done directly, as an act of emotional truth, this may be cleansing and settle the score, but it won't produce a change of consciousness.

Neutering withdrawal (FIVE): You failed to bring openly into your relationship your hope and your hunger for mutual growth and support over time; when betrayed, you turn the other way, internalize your fear of your anger and deny your hopes and expectations altogether. You were "underinvested" and now what love you had dries and dies. You deny that a problem exists; what you believe, say and have in mind is enough.

Rationalization (SEVEN): After the relationship letdown, you deny the value of the other person. You suddenly "see" the other's Shadow negative qualities, to the exclusion of other attributes. This compensates for the previous idealization you held when your ambivalence was repressed (an attitude to which SEVENS are prone) and allows you to act in a way that cuts off further contact. It often occurs after the souring of a love affair or a masculine friendship of ideas and working together.

Resentment (ONE): When your open anger is unacceptable *and* undeniable, resentment comes in; you can neither forget it, accept and swallow the insult, nor spit out the rage you feel. You tell yourself you knew all along that something like this might happen. ONES internalize anger. Consciousness narrows and thickens to hide the scars of your unacknowledged hurt.

Vindictiveness (FOUR): FOURS tend to delay and divert their desire for revenge. When it doesn't become self-pity, fantasies of cruelty or vindictiveness can take over. Your attention moves from the event of the betrayal to an obsessive, narrow focus on the person of the betrayer and her/his Shadow qualities. Consciousness shrinks to the story line you review over and over.

Manipulation (TWO): You repress knowledge of your desire for revenge, and you attempt to manipulate some gain from the situation through manifesting agitated hurt and a victim image.

Cynicism (THREE): You hide your disappointment in love, a political cause, a friend or a professional position by denying the validity of the person or the relationship, as well as denying your feelings of sadness and loss. Holding on to the images—"love is a delusion," "causes are for suckers," "therapy is brainwashing and fraud"—prevents you from working through the issues to the meaning of betrayal.

Self-blame or its opposite, paranoid projection (SIX): In the breakup of a friendship, partnership, marriage or love relationship, you find yourself looking for, and discovering, all available evidence for the same blind and sordid behavior of the other. From now on, you decide, you're going to avoid all risks. Future relationships will require loyalty oaths and constant reassurance.

Self-betrayal (NINE): In the trusted relationship you let something open up inside that you had not revealed before: a love statement, a poem, a softness. At the moment of betrayal, you allow these delicate growths to shrivel. You believe that you only got what you deserved; those inner stirrings and small rootlings were not that important after all. NINES tend to deny their core emotional response of anger. You turn off and avoid living your life phase tasks, your vocation, your own form of conscious suffering.

What do you do with this information about your feeling responses to betrayal and the defenses and Shadow issues it raises? What is the task of transformation? How do you go about it? What you originally react to as "betrayal" may be seen later, in a less emotion-laden time, as disillusionment. Disillusion is painful but necessary; all nine Enneagram types are rooted in illusion or false consciousness. The disillusion process can help us see others—and ourselves—as they really are.

For analysis, we'll use the example of two friends, Joe and Bill, who lived in a commune during their college years. Later, Joe inherited some land. He deeded over a portion of it to Bill, who had no financial prospects, but shared his vision of self-sufficient living on the land. Within three years Bill sold his portion to a developer. Joe felt betrayed.

Consciousness grows when you withstand the emotional storm of a serious moral dilemma, identify the Enneagram patterns it evokes in you and wrestle with them. Joe's task (the same task as yours, although the circumstances differ) can be described as walking the razor's edge. He had to *know* that he did not cause the betrayal. *The victim is not to blame.* He had to withstand inner and outer voices that pointed to his naive idealism, his lack of legal justification to feel victimized, as Bill now owned the land. Joe had to forgo his automatic patterns of defense. He had to contain his tension until he comprehended the meaning of the betrayal in his own life-phase learning task. He had to "forgive" *without condoning or supporting the betrayal.* In this instance, reconciliation did not happen; forgiveness simply meant not holding on to the story because that would have allowed self-poisoning. This cannot be generalized to all betrayal. Each quandary calls for its own specific active response.

Let's carry the analysis of betrayal a step further. Why should you work with such an unpleasant mirror instead of the more upbeat, interesting parts of your Enneagram style? Stress has two facets. It can reinforce your defensive patterns, but it can also reveal what needs to change, both in your psyche and in the outer situation. In an unexpected way, betrayal helps uncover the work to be done.

Each of us longs for a trusted relationship in which we see and are seen and accepted as we are, where the words we exchange are truthful and cannot be shaken. We bring this hope to our best friend, our marriage partner, our therapist. When they do not see us, when they misperceive or fail to recognize our qualities, when promises are not kept, when words that were given are broken, we feel a bitter betrayal. How paradoxical: Trust and betrayal belong together. Our betrayers are not enemies and strangers but those with whom the possibility of trust exists—parents, friends, lovers, marriage partners.

The Jungian analyst James Hillman posits that primal trust as an illusion about the outer world must be broken, not just outgrown. The broken promise or trust can become a breakthrough to another level of reality if the negative responses can be overcome.

After we have dealt with the illusions of our ego strategy, we may experience our situation in terms of a higher power, a God within or without, who also seems to betray us. Hillman probes the symbolic importance of this in the story of Jesus's three betrayals: by Judas, by Peter, and finally by God the Father. At the moment when God lets him down, Jesus becomes fully human, his pierced and wounded side releasing the fountain of life, feeling and emotion, subsequently celebrated in the Christian mysteries.[1] When inner resources seem farthest away, they turn out to be closest to us.

Betrayal, as a continuous possibility to be lived with, belongs to trust, just as doubt belongs to faith. It is the core element in the story of Abraham, the root of three major systems of faith—Judaism, Christianity and Islam. The literature that most moves us, which quickens our sense of living, deals with difficult issues and moments of choice. In working with the issues of your own life, you begin to move to a level of consciousness as different from ordinary awareness as being awake differs from sleep.

Consciousness unfolds and moves in various stages, from the "unconsciousness" of primal trust through betrayal to forgiveness by the betrayed, atonement by the betrayer, and a reconciliation by each to the event, if not necessarily to each other.[2] For all its negative aspects, there is a learning task in betrayal intimately related to our work of waking up.

We may quarrel with the view that betrayal is a necessary experience for a change in consciousness. Betrayal, like all devastating human crises, can force the moment of waking, but if the dream work and other tasks of ordinary consciousness are not done, we turn off the alarm and sink back into the sleep of our Enneagram state. On the other hand, we can also awaken naturally after we take on and complete the tasks of change, which we will now consider in Part II.

Part II:

"That you become the person only you can be"

Chapter Four:

Recovery—
Out of the Shadows

Ordinarily we think of depression, anxiety and anger as negative feelings. Better to be without feelings than have to deal with these emotions. We numb the pain with work. We escape into TV, alcohol, drugs or addictive relationships. We seldom consider the usefulness and value of these dark, difficult feelings.

Mild to moderately severe forms of depression, anxiety, and anger signal the need for closer attention. They call for action. Episodes of severe emotional disturbance—immobilizing depression, terror and rage—may require additional outside help before the person can work on his own.

Contemporary mind and brain scientists can now identify specific malfunctions in brain chemistry and associate them with a wide variety of mind states, varying from depression to love.[1]

Just as important, however, is the growing understanding of how we humans interpret and respond to felt changes in our body chemistry. For example, anxiety is a complex mental state fed from several sources—inner cellular processes and outer events. We develop theories about why we feel the way we do. These beliefs, often erroneous, can become destructive when they evolve into phobias.

Similarly, the depressed person tends to overgeneralize the meaning of events, seeing things as black and white, and feeling helpless to affect the future. This sense of helplessness is common to both endogenous (coming from a malfunction of the brain) and situational response depressions. The "learned helplessness" associated with people suffering from depression (8 million people in the United States at any one time) has interesting implications. The major factor associated with depression is inferior education, which leads to low income and the inability to attain financial security. It is a no-exit situation in a society that prizes material wealth.[2]

The solution is education, money and choices.

Submission/Depression Reframed

In the Enneagram model, escape from the limitations of a program requires facing some unpleasant reality. The difficult feelings not only allow this to happen; they bring it about. For example, in the programs of submission, the TWO finds meaning in serving the needs of an "other," a partner or a cause. When the other is lost through death, divorce or another relationship, the TWO "loses heart" and becomes dispirited. The nest empties and the life of service loses meaning. Depression forces a halt. Another relationship or cause cannot be quickly substituted. Recognizing one's own painful neediness takes priority, and a path can open out of the pattern. It is not always chosen, but the time required and the unavailability of one's usual energy allows this possibility to enter.

Similarly, the only effective interruption to the life of a successful, over-scheduled THREE is through an unavoidable failure. A desired role or goal must be lost or some personal deficit unmasked. With failure come depression and self-doubt. These may allow the performance addiction to crack and a different point of view to emerge—but only if the value of the failure is seen. The depressed, deflated feelings challenge the THREE's life direction and values.

The melancholy of the FOUR program presents a chronic addiction. Addictive depression (melancholy) is quite different from sadness and grief, which are true feelings. Addictive depression can conceal facts, reduce the sense of danger, excuse laziness, pass time and act in many other ways like a pharmaceutical "downer." It can create or maintain a condition which we do not want to see. But it also embodies a hard-won achievement over a potentially devastating early life loss. It is a construction which generates a sense of specialness hard to give up. When self-esteem plummets in a role dispute or a damaged relationship, it can trigger a real depression. When the elite image is shattered, the FOUR's ordinary human defects become apparent. The true depression reaches into the older unfinished grief and magnifies it. But the possibility of finally understanding and finishing whatever that grief requires is also present. The way out is not easily accepted.

Anxiety Reframed

We play with the edge of fear, knowing that our bodies respond with alert attentiveness to possible danger. We take in more information and focus our faculties to respond—and to flee, if necessary.

The FIVE program calls for tight boundaries and limitations in contact with the outside world. The addiction to knowledge gathering is endless. It goes beyond considerations of safety. Crisis comes when knowledge is perceived to be useless. Then the terror of facing emptiness begins. It begins in small ways—blankness, loss of memory or sense of meaning, inability to concentrate. The episodes can be momentary or last for years, as in chronic schizophrenia. The usual defenses fail against the unnamed and unknown threat. We imagine the void to mean disintegration, nothingness, non-being and death. Yet our terror points to emptiness as the only way out. Only when we gain the courage to enter the feared empty space do we find the fertile void—the space known to Taoists and artists as a source of creative solutions. It is a difficult door to choose.

The anxiety of the SIX program centers around deviance. Anything which sets the SIX apart from others makes him or her a target for jealousy, anger, criticism or whatever the SIX fears. Yet becoming a mature adult requires that we use our individual resources for independence. The strength to do this comes from exploring the edge of our fears. It comes from taking the risks Emerson identifies in his essay *Self Reliance* when he enjoins us to speak the truth lest we regret leaving things unsaid and later hearing others say them. We must speak the truth and act in a way that accords with our own insights. We must risk mistakes and loss, and risk appearing the fool. It is the way of self-discovery.

In a similar way, the endless, manipulative distractions of the SEVEN program only stop when serious pain enters one's life. The pain can be physical, emotional or mental. It concentrates attention as nothing else can. With this concentration, the pain can be read (interpreted) with different levels of meaning. Some of these directly challenge the SEVEN's control behavior patterns. Whatever is feared must be faced. It is part of the price of healing.

Anger Reframed

Everyone has to deal with anger. In Hebrew scriptures there is a saying attributed to Yahweh: "May My Mercy overcome My Wrath." Anger helps us focus on what needs to change. It also gives us the energy we need. The Enneagram programs of anger explore three modes of dealing with it as a primary force. In the EIGHT program, anger confers power to attain justice and vengeance. The problem is the lack of balance in self-defined "justice". Paradoxically, only when the EIGHT comes to understand his own weakness can the anger be directed appropriately.

The NINE program avoids conflict. Many aspects of a situation are transparently evident to the NINE so that no single position seems worth the effort of anger. Yet life requires caring choice and action. When the NINE focuses his or her anger, he can gain the energy to choose a life of greater significance.

The ONE use of anger is quite different. It takes the form of resentment which the ONE will neither discharge nor express. It prevents anything else from happening until it is properly dealt with. This entails using the anger explicitly and directly—an expression of anger which the ONE program has been constructed to avoid. So again, release from an Enneagram program starts with facing what has been avoided.

Clearly the proper use of emotion is a key element pointing to the work to be done. When emotions function properly, they allow us to meet our needs, then they subside. The chronic feelings which do not go away hang around because they are not the correct tools to do the job. We need a different feeling, but it is missing from the program we are following.

How Emotions Work

Every emotion involves a stimulus to which we respond by focusing our attention. We determine its potential threat or satisfaction and normally move into action. Our bodies respond to our strongest feelings in several ways. Our faces change to reflect the feeling; we breathe more deeply, increasing the volume of oxygen entering our lungs; we express the feeling in sounds. When we allow a feeling to sweep through us, we moan, holler, laugh, scream or grunt. Then, at the height of the feeling, a reflexive action of the spine occurs. A strong ripple runs through the spinal column producing the pelvic

thrust of orgasm, the gagging motion of vomiting, the rocking movement of grief and of convulsive laughter, the movements of rage and
terrified flight.

We have to let out and discharge our strongest feelings of rage,
terror, grief, sexuality and hilarity. It is as if they would poison our
bodies if held in. Many feelings are not this intense. We can express
them in a less global fashion, sometimes just with the twitch of a
cheek muscle and the flicker of an eye. However, when we chron-
ically block any feeling, it is as if we clogged a pipeline; all feelings
have difficulty getting through, and the unexpressed feelings deaden
our bodies and spirits.

Blocking Emotional Responses

Think of what a little boy looks like when he's trying not to cry:
shoulders stiff, mouth tight, chin tucked in, barely breathing, while
he holds his eyes wide so the tears won't slip out. When, for
whatever reason, it seems dangerous to us to express one or more
of our feelings, we block the movement of our spine, hold our breath,
stop any sound and mask our facial expression. As we do this over
time, the blocking instructions settle into our muscles and connective
tissue. The result is that, in preventing ourselves from expressing
one feeling, we have more difficulty feeling and letting go of any.
They all use the same physical pathways. Recovery releases the body.

Spontaneous feeling is one thing, forms of expression another.
Even as we must weed, water and fertilize a garden, we need to
cultivate feelings to develop their powers. Feelings develop in
appropriate terrains, a range of situations to which each belongs. In
sorting through our feelings, weeding out misplaced and wandering
emotions from other areas in our life, we develop a stronger, more
accurate sense of what is going on and how we should respond.

One of the Enneagram weeds that infest feelings is an addiction to "highs," the overstimulation of a desired phase of feeling.
For example, people often look for incidents to feed their rage, and
the expression of rage is very contagious. Cultivating feelings requires
learning which ones need to be weeded, and addictions are the
obvious candidates. An addiction to the highs of sex, violence, terror
and various destructive relationships hides the subtler satisfactions
of feeling completed and satisfied. It wants to fix a moment in time
rather than to allow the natural rhythmic flow of a feeling. Like the

physical saturation of drug or alcohol addiction, emotional saturation requires more and more stimulation to achieve the same effects. A growing appetite for violence and sexuality is a gross substitute for educated feeling. Other emotional addictions function as tranquilizers and promise escape.

Undoubtedly, the codes of proper behavior that humankind has been inventing since the dawn of time are based on the judgment that feelings have to be appropriately expressed to function well. Nevertheless, in our fear of developing emotional situations which we cannot deal with, we construct not only conscious codes of behavior, but also the unconscious Enneagram defenses against knowing which feelings are really there.

Projection and Recovery

Projection is a common and complex response: denying a particular feeling in ourselves and sensing it as coming from the other person. It resembles the way we forget the movie projector and focus our attention on the image coming from the screen.

In projection, we do not perceive nor do we intend to transfer these feelings in us which are difficult to know and accept. The other person always has some little "hook" on which we can hang the projected feeling. The presence of the hook allows us to magnify its evidence and ignore our own matching quality.

For example, Paul borrows his older brother Bill's car and scrapes a fender. Bill is irritated (the hook). If Paul projects his own jealous anger onto Bill, he may magnify the evidence of irritation and experience his brother as hating him and wanting to embarrass him in front of his friends. He can feel justified in his view that Bill is selfish and doesn't deserve an apology, much less amends. Then Paul doesn't have to recognize or deal with his jealous anger.

Now comes one of our most important human characteristics. We seem to have a drive to know what is true. In certain phases of inner development, the same unconscious which generated the projections also strives to correct them.

Five Steps in Withdrawal of Projection

1. *Projection:* When we believe what we believe is so.
2. *Doubt Denied:* Some information doesn't quite fit, but "louder and wronger," we insist it is so.

3. *Recognition:* "Small and ugly" self-blame for wrong perception.

4. *Empathy:* We can see the other's point of view.

5. *Assimilation:* We shift to include the complexity of feeling two ways about something/someone.

In this train of events, projection (when we absolutely believe what we believe is so) is the first step toward assimilating unpalatable information. We need this information, but we must alter it before we can digest it. In this phase, we believe that *the other person* is the one who is angry, can't be trusted and will take every advantage to put us down (or whatever difficult feeling that we are not owning).

Now, either we become aware that not everybody sees the other person as we do, or we notice that we always seem to view a particular type of person in the same way. It occurs to us that maybe we are using a screen.

> When Kate was a young social worker, it occurred to her that perhaps she was unduly pressuring young, unmarried mothers to give up their babies for adoption. Maybe this was related more to her unresolved issues with her own mother than to the needs of her clients. When Mickey entered the Army and found himself dealing with black men for the first time, he began to wonder if the things he had assumed about them were true.

This second phase is not a comfortable time. We have an investment in our point of view; we do not want to admit that we may be wrong. If we are particularly well-tuned into our bodies, we may even find we feel a bit like throwing up. It takes courage and integrity to stay with the difficult new hunch.

It becomes easier when we gain a sense of empathy with others and try to see their circumstances from their point of view. Then we can take the next step of recognition: What we have believed does not exist in the way we thought it did. Marie-Louise von Franz, a famous Swiss psychoanalyst who has written extensively on projection, calls this the small and ugly phase. We're embarrassed. *God! I've been doing this awful thing for all this time. Probably everyone has seen that I'm the one who is angry and attacking, not he. How could I have been so blind?* Physically, we feel dismayed and empty.[3]

In the final step, assimilation, we consciously own the feeling point of view we projected onto the other. As this happens, a shift takes place, because we have to include the complexity and tension of feeling two ways about something: We can love and be angry, be angry and be fearful, and have other seemingly contradictory feelings. The context is no longer black and white. It has an interesting texture and fullness.

> Once Kate gave up her projection that single mothers were hanging on to their infants when the babies were better off in adoptive homes, she could finally see her personal problem: how to separate from her own mother and claim her own point of view without using hate and rejection as a false means to make the separation. She could see that the unmarried mothers did not all need to separate from their babies. Each mother's difficulty had its own particular issues and feelings. When Mickey gave up his projections on black men, he could experience them as men like himself with the same hungers and needs for recognition.

Because we now know ourselves to be people who can be bigoted, who can act in blind, hateful, fearful and other intolerable ways, we astonishingly become people who can be more tolerant and accepting of the stumbling, limited mistake-making people who surround us. We forgive ourselves. We regain the energy lost in the original projection and we are back to feeling curious and interested in whatever is occurring—with fewer screens.

The Enneagram Process Toward Integration and Health

As we take back our projections and recognize our biases, defenses and screened projections, we lighten our programming. We find it easier to understand another person's frame of reference. We can move with empathy into their point of view and toward a more complex, profound understanding of objective reality. As Flannery O'Connor put it, "Everything that rises must converge." The illustration represents this movement toward an integrated point of one consciousness, corresponding to Teilhard de Chardin's Omega Point. Conversely, the more stuck we are, the more separate.

A War Within of Opposite Feelings

Other situations can call out mixtures of feelings which sometimes horrify us. For example, when someone close to us dies, we find it quite difficult to admit the anger, resentment and even disgust we feel. Yet these feelings are a normal part of loss. We can feed an urgent need to get the loved one back and to scold her or him for leaving us. No matter how irrational or inappropriate this seems, only when the tension of these emotions is felt and discharged can we move on. The same thing can happen when a relationship breaks up. Even with the delicious, loving feelings of a parent for a child, an admixture of hostility, even hatred, can intrude. Feelings evoked in us when we become parents have a great deal in common with the feelings called out in us by our own parents and other family members of the past. The small infant can trigger in the parent possessiveness, jealousy and antagonism for the baby's demanding ways. The task is to admit, tolerate and regulate these feelings—not to deny them.

The interplay of emotions that we found at the individual level in the Enneagram also operates in group and community processes, with the same types of costs and the possibility of resolution.

Reframing is the essence of a fourth tactic for dealing with threat. It is an artful, human alternative to the Enneagram strategies of fighting, fleeing, or submitting. It is absolutely necessary in dealing with Shadow issues, both personal and collective.

Levels of Conflict and Reframing

Level of Conflict	Defensive Response	Healing Tactic (deals with projection— moves to negotiation)
Inner psyche: blow to self-esteem	Deny, rationalize, project, displace.	Not defend, but reframe and shift point of view, accept information—which allows inclusion and leads to transformation.
Interpersonal: self vs. other	1. Feel angry, fight. 2. Feel anxious, flee. 3. Submit, feel depressed.	Shift point of view, role reverse; with each strong emotion, include its opposite; pay attention to what is not included—which allows us to reframe conflict and negotiate.
Within the group: true believers vs. scapegoat or rebel	1. Fight. 2. Flee/distract to fight an outer enemy; unify "us" by fighting "them." 3. Submit to "groupthink;" suppress individual doubt and data.	Shift point of view; *Cui bono?* ("Who benefits?" "Follow the money"); value doubt and ambiguity— which allows us to reframe conflict and negotiate.
Inter-group/ Inter-nation: "Us" vs. "them"	1. "Take 'em to court"; make war. 2. Make war with enemy's minor ally. 3. Lose face.	Identify common bonds, common threats, and work to identify reciprocity; pay attention to what is *not* happening. Value ambiguity—which allows us to reframe conflicts and negotiate.

Political and conflict-solving skills can be taught. The column of healing tactics contains several implications. First, every relation is reciprocal. What we say of "them," they can say of "us," and vice versa. (This is a version of owning our own projections. When we are irritated by others, we irritate others as well.) We place ourselves in our opponents' shoes and see their points of view.

Second, we look for opposites within the opponent or opposing group—and within ourselves or our own group. When any strong emotion is present, the opposite is also there in some way: love and hate, anger and fear, pain and pleasure, control and impulsiveness, self-righteousness and guilt, low self-esteem and grandiosity. If a person expresses hatred and rage, we can also explore how he also loves and wants a relationship with the one he is raving about. Very often we push away the thing or person we want most for fear that we cannot have it or, once we have it, cannot keep it. A strong statement invites further exploration. "Leave me alone," often covers "don't go," even as "everything's wonderful" attempts to conceal "things are not okay." For every occurence, its opposite also occurs at some other time or in some other respect.

These oppositions are fundamental energies. Each of the Enneagram strategies includes oppositions (such as the ONE's drive to perfection together with the resentment that accompanies awareness of a lack of perfection or the TWO's stance of helpfulness with inattention to personal needs). We can examine any circumstance and learn how the oppositions work, what they allow to happen and to whose benefit.

Third, we pay attention to what did not happen, what isn't being said, and what is not being done. Explicit denial and absence are two forms of negation.

These three actions, which lead to reframing conflict, imply a willingness to enter into a face-to-face process. But it is often difficult to get groups to take the first step of sitting down together. Political skill means trying one thing, then another, in finding what works. Sometimes it requires the craft of community organizing.

The business community has developed some techniques for conflict resolution that need to be more widely known. They use group facilitators, recorders and representatives from the different factions involved, while they solve problems and introduce new ideas into the corporate culture. Another powerful tool, "single text negotiation," helps opponents write a mutually agreeable contract or treaty. From corporate headquarters to Soviet-American summits, the single text technique has shifted from the adversarial approach toward cooperative mediation of shared problems.

Turning opposing power forces to problem solving is complex. We have to decide to fight with words, not weapons and sabotage. Instead of tearing into each other, we listen carefully, work bit by bit, and wait for consensus about action plans. We take events apart and look for connections. As the issues unfold we have to deal with our own feelings of rage and despair, deception and sometimes betrayal. If we endure and work with these emotions, instead of regarding them as ends in themselves, resolution results.

Enneagram Types of Leadership

In integration, the type of leadership needed for change and wholeness does not come initially from power leaders interested in dominance and control (the ONE, THREE and EIGHT strategies), but must develop from the initiatives of the relationship leaders, people skilled at hearing feelings (the TWO, FOUR and SIX strategies) and visionary leaders, people skilled at reframing, seeing new possibilities (the FIVE, SEVEN and NINE strategies). These leaders, by definition relatively weak, often don't realize they are leaders of a different kind. For example, the recent steps toward nuclear arms reduction have come about only because millions of seemingly powerless people have joined in protests throughout the world.

In this chapter we have looked at the value of our most difficult feelings. We have considered how emotions function normally and the importance of access to the full range of our feelings. We have reframed difficult feelings as pointing to a way out of addictive Enneagram programs. We have explored their use in situations of group conflict. Finally we have considered the types of leadership the Enneagram can develop as its tasks are solved. In the next section we move beyond the problems of the Enneagram to changing levels of consciousness.

Chapter Five:

Moving On

Changing Levels of Consciousness

When we recover the range of our feelings, we are ready to move into deeper, wider, more intense states of awareness. We already know two states, being asleep and being awake. Sleep has various phases. During some, we sift, sort and symbolize our experiences in the images of dreams. We also apparently prepare for creative shifts that will take place in our more awake state.[1] But "being awake" covers a wide range of states of awareness.

A great amount of "perception," information processing and decision making can take place without consciousness or awareness. When we study hypnosis and psychological conditioning, we realize how pervasive these influences are.

Just as we can sleep deeply, then lightly towards morning, ordinary consciousness has its own deeper and lighter states. Alcohol, drugs, television and any of our Enneagram addictive pre-occupations create the deeper hypnotic and conditioned states of ordinary consciousness. On the other hand, whenever we cut down the incessant input of data and allow our questioning mind to awake, our programmed consciousness lightens. By emphasizing silence and quieting the mind in meditation, we can "tune up" our senses so that inner information, usually overwhelmed, gets through.

Whenever we pause to question something that's "obvious," whenever a poem touches our hearts, or a piece of art or music opens an insight, our state of ordinary consciousness lightens. We move to wake.

Most of the world's work is done while we are functioning in ordinary consciousness, but a more objective awareness is possible. There is as much difference between objective consciousness and ordinary consciousness as there is between ordinary consciousness and sleep. In ordinary consciousness, we are not aware of the inconsistencies and contradictions of our experience. For example, practically no one questions the peculiarities of a concept like "ownership." We seldom think of mysteries like life, suffering and death. We gloss over, or screen out, any data that do not support our Enneagram state.

Ordinary consciousness might be thought of as a semi-trance state into which we were inducted by our culture in infancy. Our parents, our schooling, our "way of life" all reinforce its suggestions, so most of the time we exist in complete agreement with the people around us that this is the way things are. We glimpse this conditioning when we think of enclaves "different from us" like fundamentalist Moslems, urban slum children dealing drugs, or the mentally ill, but we do not easily see ourselves in this light.

When we recover our feelings, we begin to increase our consciousness. We notice that there are other kinds of awareness.

Waking From Ordinary Consciousness

Stories of journeying—going on a quest to find a treasure and finding one's true identity as a result—are found in all cultures and in all periods of history. Although dogmatic beliefs and cultural misunderstandings obscure much of what has been found, agreement remains that there are steps or stages to the journey. The mystics of Christianity and Judaism, the Sufis of Islam, Buddhists and followers of other Eastern religions all describe the steps in remarkably similar ways. Some systems of psychology and several epics of literature also embody their principles. We need special training which reaches beyond the conscious self to the inner self. Our habit patterns need transformation. Objective consciousness requires more levels of awareness operating at the same time with our self-awareness.

To picture the state of objective consciousness, imagine listening to an orchestra. You can hear the melody of the woodwinds, the different but complementary melodic lines of the horns and other instruments. You are aware of the shape of the music, how it is unfolding and where it is tending. Attention can operate in a similar multileveled way to include one's natural setting, one's body sensations, the flow of emotional responses to and from other people, the basic direction, eddies and ripples of thought. In such a situation, consciousness itself seems to flow, not from one place to another, but rather as a felt unity that is "everywhere and nowhere."

Rigidly fixed ideas obstruct this flow. The Enneagram is one way of describing the constricted programs which prevent us from moving out on a path of knowledge.

We begin at our state of discontent. We wish for greater meaning, but breaking loose from the habits of a lifetime brings periods of intense anxiety, confusion and occasional panic. Some people start out alone, often in prayer, but others need a form of psychotherapy or a spiritual discipline to identify the beginning work.

Choosing a Path

Many paths invite us. The important thing is to choose one particular discipline and do it wholeheartedly for a long enough period of time that it has a chance to affect us.

Exploring other paths has value and can serve to reframe our questions, allowing them to be seen freshly, but working within our own religious and cultural traditions is less difficult. Our collective images, language and understandings steep through our consciousness. They interlace our dreams and thoughts. In the Western world, many of these images come from Greek and Roman myths and the Old and New Testaments. It is not easy for us to discriminate the subtle images, language patterns and allusions at work in the religious disciplines of another culture.

Once we have chosen a path, we should follow it. If little happens, if the practice doesn't produce the expected results, we should consciously stop it. We may not be ready to do it properly. If we ever want to come back to it in a serious way, it won't have lost its potential for being half-tried.

Use of a Guide

Eastern and Western traditions agree that at some point it is useful to work on our path with a guide. However, it is important to know the boundaries and limits of that relationship.

Our need to know ourselves through another's eyes starts in infancy and runs throughout our lives. We need to feel seen and cared about as we are. We express the need in attachment to a trusted other. With this relationship as a secure base, our survival energy is free to be used in investigating our environment, in making our own discoveries, and in forming other relationships. We are free to become ourselves with often quite different thoughts and attitudes from that trusted other. (Nietzsche remarked that if a teacher's students never disagreed with him, he had failed as a teacher.)

Good parents provide that type of experience in childhood. If they did not, then a secure relationship in later life can fill our needs. Many people who work with a spiritual director or who are "in therapy" temporarily use the director or therapist as such a figure. This allows them sufficient security that they can explore their lives and experiment with other forms of intimacy. They do not need the therapist's knowledge so much as the safe relationship, which allows them to explore and find their own questions, their own values, and their own individual views of "reality." Similarly, therapy groups can become a laboratory to use in experimenting with new behaviors, feelings and attitudes. Other self-help groups, including religious groups and those which practice silence together, can serve the same function.

Clearing Out Old Programs

The spiritual path requires encounter with our own dark side and what we have programmed ourselves to avoid. Beginning to know and acknowledge our negative traits and qualities involves a deep and extended flushing out of underground emotions, memories and motives which inhibit the use of our full capacities and distort how we see things.

By definition, the screens of the Enneagram strategies are what we are trying to rid ourselves of. The next section offers a possible way of approaching this task.

Chapter Six:

A Program of Individual Work

The only thing you need to do is become the person only you can be.

The monk-poet Thomas Merton said, "If you want to identify me...ask me what I think I am living for, in detail, and ask me what I think is keeping me from living fully for the thing I want to live for."[1] If you use these questions, you may find that they lead to deepening or changing your own life direction.

The program which follows outlines a series of written journal exercises to help you explore these questions. You might find it useful to include some non-verbal work, art processes and active imagination methods, as these offer other types of understanding. The sequence is adapted from a residential program of intensive therapy, to fit a personal journal.[2]

I have included italicized notes in the following two segments, *Here and Now* and *The Family Sculpture*, and later. They indicate the thoughts of a psychotherapist working with a client on this material and are intended to demystify the process of therapy. The reader can decide whether this type of assistance might be useful to her or him.

Here and Now

In your journal, write what occurs to you in response to Merton's question. What are you living your life for? What disturbs you sufficiently that you want to undertake this exploration?

As a psychotherapist, I spend the first session listening in silence to the person's story. I listen to how she tells the story, the power of the verbs and the amount of energy in the metaphors and images. I listen to the body language and the senses used to encode information, like "I see" or "the thing didn't smell right." I listen for relationship pushes and pulls, discomfort and hope. These are the energies for change. What is this person wanting, hoping will happen? Where is she in the life cycle and how has she dealt with the preceding tasks? What is the sticking place, what is this person avoiding? I may use questions to increase or lessen the discomfort, to offer hope or lessen unrealistic expectation.

Unfinished Business From the Past: Family Legacy Questions

Because you tend to recreate the unfinished issues of your early family life in your current relationships, unconsciously hoping to resolve them, it is useful to identify these issues clearly. The best exercise I know is the family sculpture.[3] It offers an entry to the Enneagram in that it identifies the dominant feeling—depression, anxiety or anger—and the personal stance. *The personal stance phrase can be thought of as a summary of script decisions.* The description which follows includes an example of a man who has chosen an Enneagram SIX strategy: security dominated by fear and doubt.

The family sculpture is a directed meditation which results in a clay model of earliest relationships. It contains clues to problems in the present and how to work with them. Unspoken family assumptions in the form and placement of clay figures becomes objectively visible.

Analysis of a family sculpture focuses on four levels: the family of origin, the projection level, the introjection level, and the possibilities of change in the present. The art medium can be plastic or potter's clay.

When you were a child, you received a lot of messages and instructions from your family about how to be you. You learned how to behave, how to please and upset your parents. You also picked up some of their attitudes toward life, particularly their view of your importance or lack of it. One way to explore these messages is by sculpting how your family felt to you when you were growing up. You are investigating how you came to think of yourself in the ways you do.

First, think back to a time in childhood before you started school. Who was around? How old were they? Include all family members and grandparents, as well as pets or neighbors if they were special to you. Note on paper two or three adjectives describing each person, then take the clay and make a *sculpture of the adjectives* which describe one particular person. The idea is not to make a figure of the person but something that gives you a feeling of how that person felt to you when you were younger.

When you have sculpted each family member in turn, including yourself, put them in relation to one another to show who seemed close to you and who was emotionally far away.

Note on paper the messages you received from each family member. Use strongly worded, brief sentences for both the action messages and the things they said to you.

Write the decisions you made as a result of how this family felt to you while you were growing up.

When analysis is done in a group, it is interesting to invite the group to relate just to the sculptural feeling of each figure and to comment on the "obvious," such things as the relative size and placement of the figures and similarities in shape. Insight can emerge for the one making the sculpture who has not seen what seems obvious to others. For example, when the figures line up "stage front" and do not interact with each other so much as with an unseen audience, family values become apparent which emphasize "how we look to others" over "how we feel in relation to each other." I mention to the group that each observer "sees" different things in the sculpture which accord with his own preoccupations.

Family sculpting allows inner knowledge of one's plight, whether conscious or not, to become visible. Almost invariably, the figure occupying the central place in the sculpture has the power position in the family. Usually this is a parent but sometimes a more favored brother or sister. When the one creating the sculpture places herself in the center, she acknowledges power. When the creator "forgets" to include himself, the omission is always based on a feeling which needs to be known.

Tell your story—how you felt, growing up in this family.

As therapist, I listen carefully to the descriptive words and phrases the person uses. These descriptive words can also be thought of as major elements in the client's world model. I also pay attention to what the client avoids. "Racket" feelings get substituted for forbidden feelings. The resulting impasse is often apparent in the family figures.

Analysis of the Family Sculpture

The Projective Level

We often choose to be with people who feel familiar and "seem like family." For example, adult children of alcoholics tend to find one another, as do those who have experienced other kinds of abuse. The unique complex of attitudes, feelings, and avoidances identified in a family sculpture is much like a language for the individual; we tend to gravitate towards people who speak a similar tongue. Sometimes the original correspondence between friends' or partners' emotional language is not so great. As they learn how to please and hurt one another, the partners recognize and reinforce familiar patterns (both positive and negative). We sometimes fail to recognize that people treat us in the same ways that we were treated by family members in the past, because we tend to recreate situations with the same themes and "unfinished business;" for example, a man's competitive rivalry with a sister may be re-enacted with a series of women.

Who in your present life is sending you messages that sound like those you used to hear from your parents and other family members?

We often experience parental messages coming from hierarchical relationships: a boss at work or an institution such as our profession or church. Relationships with brothers and sisters may be re-enacted with peers, clients or one's children. Many family-of-origin messages, positive and negative, may now be experienced as coming from our marriage partner.

The Introjective Level

How many of these messages do you also experience as coming from yourself—what you tell yourself, or how you judge yourself?

In the introjective level of analysis, messages once experienced as coming from outside persons are now perceived as what one tells oneself. A parent's injunction, "work hard," has become one's self-description, "I'm a hard worker, maybe even a workaholic."

The Redecision Level

This level of analysis focuses on the possibilities for change in one's present life.

When you look at the shape you have given your mother figure and see her as "clutching," "loving," "fragile" (or whatever description

you've used), what do you feel was missing for her in her life? W
did she need in order to function effectively, or feel understood a..u
supported? Was there someone in the family who could have
understood and helped? What stood in the way? What does this
correspond to as your inner reality?

Moving the figures about, without changing their forms, shows
the way the family used and avoided using power. Clues emerge
to issues that the person is ready to work on.

Diagnosis is a shorthand description of a person's dilemma. It
includes injunctions and decisions, but also the person's assets,
strengths and capacity to redecide, change those early decisions,
and deal with his current life. His motivation, discomfort, hope and
the realistic possibilities that circumstances and the therapeutic
encounter offer, influence these redecisions.

Redecisions result from conscious appraisal of one's current life,
current abilities, and strength to choose more satisfying ways of living.

The family sculpture provides a vivid picture of the person's
earliest world model. His or her unique resources, legacy of emotions, beliefs and behavior become visible. Acceptable and hidden
values, helpful and limiting decisions about power, personal worth
and sexuality can be drawn from it. Feeling knowledge often
bypasses the conscious mind to appear in the clay forms. Distortions from the past, evident in the sculpture, contain clues to
problems in the present and how to work with them. Discussions
of the sculpture can focus the redecision work. Redecisions result
from conscious appraisal of one's current life, current abilities, and
strength to choose more satisfying ways of living.

What do you want to change in your life? What must you do
first to allow this to happen? How will you go about it? When?

*As a therapist, I use this redecision work to develop the contract—the
agreement between myself and my client on what we are going to do together,
how we will proceed, how long it will take, and the changes which will
signal that our work is finished.*

Case Analysis: The Family Sculpture of Jake, a middle-aged furniture designer

Mother: alcoholic, indifferent, displaying occasional warmth and humor

Father: loyal, cautious, tightfisted

Jake: "easy-going but not going anywhere"

Sister: bright, angry, competitive

Levels of Analysis:

1. *The "Obvious:"*
The central place and size of the sister.
The father as a small formless lump.
The mother's engulfing, cavelike quality.
A design similarity between Jake's figure and the mother's.

2. *Family-of-Origin Messages:*
(Father) "Life will disappoint you, so don't aim too high."
(Mother) "I can't be around for you. Don't be a bother."
(Sister) "Who needs you? I'll get my own."

Translated into Program decisions: Go for security. Don't take risks. Don't be close. Don't be important.

Jake's Enneagram Program of security seeking was evident in his history. The "good boy" in his family, Jake never lost his temper and worked as hard as he thought he was capable. His father, who drifted from job to job, modeled "not aiming too high" and "not making it." The mother supported the family by working in a fish market. Jake added what he could earn from paper and delivery routes.

In entering therapy, Jake feared he might be following in his father's path. He had failed to get into architecture school because he became "confused" under pressure. His furniture design business failed, although he thought he had some talent. He was now employed in an office job below even his own low assessment of his abilities, but it was "secure." Always feeling on the brink of failure left him little time for personal life and the latest of a series of women with whom he was marginally involved had just left him to marry someone else. This prompted him to "try therapy."

3. *Projective Level of Analysis:*

The relationship issues in Jake's family of origin were repeated in his own life and choice of partners on whom he could project his sister's message, "Who needs you? I'll get my own." He enacted his mother's "Don't be close" with would-be friends and he accepted his father's "Don't aim too high, you won't make it" by failing in his business.

4. *Introjective Level:*

Jake was aware that he was responsible for the lack of intimacy in his life, and he admitted that an inner voice told him that he did not amount to much. He wanted to try another business venture, but it filled him with apprehension. He did not identify with his sister's anger, but he sometimes felt he did have talent and could make it as she had.

5. *Psychotherapy Contract:*

Redecision to aim higher, to make it and to be close to someone. This meant *using* therapy instead of "trying" it, staying with whatever feelings were struggling to be heard in back of the "confusion," taking risks in entering business for himself again and taking on a new relationship. He decided six months would be sufficient time to reprogram himself.

Risking expression of his feelings in a therapy group, Jake found his anger which had never been available to him in relationships. He found it useful (almost destroyed by his joy at feeling it) in both his job and relationships. At the end of the contract period, he had quit his office job, obtained a small business loan and was setting up a promising business. He decided that a further three-month period of therapy to deal with his deepening feelings was in order.

Establishing the family script uses your thinking intellect. It gives you a map and shows the best access routes. To change your Enneagram program, however, you need to work your feelings out. That involves the use of two other types of intellect: your emotional evaluation and your body's instinctive reactions. People differ in their access to these evaluation processes and some of your work will be to awaken these skills.

Finishing Family Issues

The unexpressed feelings of childhood still press to be known. This does not mean that you must say them to your living parent. The parent of your childhood who angered or saddened you is long gone. When dealing with these feelings, the support and objectivity of another person, or other people, helps.

A place to begin is with your journal. Note whatever memories you have from each of the first twelve years of your life. As an adult today, how do you see the child you were? What were the child's needs? What feelings did the child block from expression—fear, anger, sadness? Allow yourself to identify with that child's feelings again, and give them a voice by writing them in your journal in the form of a letter to your parent of the past.

Every child needs to be loved and cared for, to have a secure base from which he or she can move out, explore his world and become himself. When this is taken away or unavailable, the child is hurt.

Many aspects of our suffering occur in strong, emotional states of consciousness. We try to deal with the consequences in ordinary consciousness, e.g., try to get at the root of a fear by talking about it. Often we don't succeed because the remedy is specific to the state of heightened emotion. We only gain access to irrational fear in the state of fearfulness.

The methods of psychodrama, recreating scenes from the past, reversing roles with problematic parents and partners, and working through the issues, offer the strongest means of feeling catharsis. The support of a therapist and the psychodrama group allows you to experience the difficult feelings while also feeling protected and cared for. Working with your journal, you can review the needs of the child you once were and the decisions that child made. You can now make some redecisions about your current life.

A journal exercise, when you have finished your redecision work, is taken in the shoes of your most problematic parent. You are to write an autobiography using his or her voice, as if you were that parent. Tell your story, describe your experiences and problems with your parents, what you wanted to become when you were an adolescent, your dreams and what happened to them. Describe how you came to choose your marriage partner and how you felt about conceiving this child (the one doing the journal work). What was going on around the time of his or her birth? What did you hope for his or her future? How do you see the difficulties that have come between you?

When you are sure you have a good sense of your parent's feelings through doing this "autobiography," go for a walk and think about what has happened to your perception of the family. Write what else occurs to you.

You may now want to write something of your other feelings: your forgiveness, your gratitude, or (if your parents are still a part of your life) issues you know you will never agree on, and how you plan to deal with them. If you feel completely blocked on some matter, think of the wisest person possible who also cares deeply for you. Imagine consulting that person about the feeling block and write the answer as it forms in your mind, sentence by sentence. Write until you feel closure and you have finished the issues with your parent.

It is important to use the empathy you gain with your parent's difficulties to express your gratitude for life and whatever that parent wanted to give to you. Unexpressed appreciation is as big a block to life as any other feeling.

Anthony de Mello, a Jesuit writer, says that it is impossible to feel depressed and grateful at the same time.[4]

Now, do the other parent.

Current Matters: Your Sub-Personalities

When you have finished with these past issues, you are better prepared to understand your current quandary. A place to begin is in identifying your inner conflicts by visualizing different drives within you as sub-personalities. For example, you could imagine nine parts within you corresponding to the Enneagram strategies and give each a voice to discuss something of concern to you. You get a fresh perspective with alternative ways of looking at the matter.

Start with your familiar inner aspects. You probably have noticed that you behave in different ways in different situations and with different people. Occasionally, you're aware that you hold two points of view or desires that seem to contradict each other. Various writers recognize these inner splits. Fritz Perls, in gestalt psychology, called the two major parts of the personality, usually found opposing one another, topdog and underdog. The particular character and concerns vary from person to person, but topdog always has very definite opinions about what underdog "should" be doing. In literature, Stevenson's *Dr. Jekyll and Mr. Hyde* points to this same underlying dichotomy.

People who know you in only one set of circumstances might be astonished if they saw you at home. You act differently. Parts of you enter into each of these relationships differently from the others: perhaps a sexuality with your partner that is not visible to your children, or a "touchiness" with your parent that is not called out when you're with your partner. You occasionally experience an inner impasse while two opposing forces within you struggle for expression. It is important not to identify with any one of these "selves" and to recognize that each is a role you play.

Enneagram ego-state descriptions simply indicate the dominant personality. You have less developed aspects and creative, spontaneous parts which come from the deeper Self. So also include your sub-personalities, and give them a voice. The work you have done in finishing issues with your family may have prepared the way for changes in these inner characters.

After completing your cast of characters, envision calling them together for a meeting in which all have their say. The first item on the agenda is "What is your role in the way I am living my life, what do you need, what do you like to do, and how often do you get to do it? What is the price of change that you fear to pay?" You might add to the agenda problems in relationships, career issues and choices, and whatever else concerns you.

You're the chairperson and the choice maker, but this device of consulting your sub-personalities helps to surface your different desires, inner oppositions and where they are coming from.

Autobiography

An exercise that may take several weeks is to write your own autobiography in seven-year segments. In roughly seven-year periods, your body changes significantly and you face new developmental tasks. Before you write each segment, make notes. What was that period about? Who were the important people in it for you? What questions did you have to solve? What issues troubled you? What did you learn, what strengths did you gain?

Here and Now—Again

Take the autobiography and, with paper and crayons or other art materials, sketch a life line. Show the turning points, the people who were important to you, and the times and places when your attention shifted to new goals. Mark the place where you are now and continue the line to the time you expect to die. What choices do you face now: psychological, physical, spiritual, economic, social, community and political? What condition do you want to be in five years from now; what work and relationships do you want in your life? When you come to die, what will you want your life to have included?

Advanced Work

The first act of your life script has been played, your Enneagram strategy chosen. It's one of your "givens," and establishes some of the boundaries of your drama. You can revise the second act, however, depending on how you want the play to go.

The temptation is to look for expert help. It helped to have a guide or a set of exercises to do when you were investigating the early script. The problem with this is that the skills needed now are solo, and you have to act in the play as you acquire them. You have to understand how your psychological character works; then you have to develop a genuinely awake and knowledgeable part of your mind to play the part and unfold the meanings you desire.

Enneagram Exercises

Work with an Enneagram group provides useful mirrors. If this is not feasible, you might work with a friend in a series of "talks." These are not dialogues or discussions. Each person takes fifteen minutes to talk continuously on one aspect of the Enneagram cluster of characteristics, such as the TWO issue of avoidance of one's own needs. You explore how you experience this in your life, how it makes you feel, the side effects and whatever else occurs to you. Your partner listens attentively, but makes no response with words, sounds or body movement directed to you. When you have finished, you act as listener to your partner. When this concludes, you can share your feelings about the experience and what you discovered about yourself in using this discipline (continuous talk and non-response listening).

Do only one topic in any given meeting; when you meet again, move on to the next facet of the Program—for example, the TWO's issue of manipulation in relationships. Your experience will deepen in your observations. You progress through all the issues of each program.

Your study of the Enneagram has provided a place to begin, but understanding your character comes with self-observation. Entering and revising the drama entails developing the skill of double consciousness, or self-remembering while you do the ordinary work of your life.

Obstacles to the work of self-observation include lack of motivation (discomfort or hope), lack of skill, distraction and active resistance. Our culture does not encourage self-observation. "There's work to be done." "You ought to relax." "There's an interesting TV program on." "Shouldn't you stop being so heavy and concerned with yourself all the time?"

Self-observation requires a resolution to "know what is so, regardless of how I wish it to be." It requires patience—and the rest of your life. It's hard work, but your interest intensifies as you realize that there are side effects. You are paying acute attention to four levels of data: your emotional awareness, your body responses, your intellectual focus and your intuitive curiosity about the linkages you observe.

The gestalt Awareness Continuum is a good place to begin. You might work with a tape recorder, or take turns with another person. The idea is to say whatever enters your awareness from your body sensations and your senses—sounds, visual impressions, scents. Try to observe every thought, feeling, image or connection that comes along. It is important to be totally non-selective. Let each thought or image be itself, evolving as it wishes. Let it pass in its own way. Do not deliberately hold any experience. Don't identify with it or deny it. Just let the stream flow while you pay full attention to it. Notice your thinking as such—for example, that you have left your senses and are thinking about, remembering, fantasizing or making comparisons and lists of what you should be doing.

When we were young, "should" had an outer-directed sense, meaning for our own good, roughly to gain pleasure and avoid pain. Now that we've outgrown this dichotomy, it means behaving according to our vision of maximizing some more subtle good than pleasure. But in stress, we go back to the outer demand use of "should."

Self-observation is not self-analysis. It's like gathering data in science. You are grounding yourself in primary data to acquire objective clarity. Sometimes a small image, barely glimpsed, can provide a stunning insight.

In the double consciousness of self-remembering, you are working toward a more unified consciousness. Your knowledge skills are fragmented, not all that ready for whatever comes. Here you are expanding your awareness to include several levels at the same time: body instincts, feeling responses and intellectual knowledge to promote integrated functioning.

Attention is something like a flabby muscle. You can strengthen it through exercise.

Silence and "Yes"

Whether they define their purpose as finding a greater consciousness, a fuller sense of reality or a path to God, increasing numbers of people have added the practice of silence to their spiritual discipline. As Anthony de Mello says, "The way to God must pass through silence, going beyond words and thoughts."[5]

You can use your imaginative power to discover what you worship. It may be different from what you think you worship. The systems analyst C. West Churchman says that the religious approach to human affairs occurs first when you decide there is something you regard as superior, grander, more magnificent than you feel yourself to be. You act because you feel that you should conform to the superior being's intentions or existence, or because your actions are forms of worship. "The superior being may be many things...a personalized deity, 'Nature', community and everything-nothing."[6] He points out that our society worships both large technologies and the economy, capricious deities which may collapse and do dreadful things if we do not appease them. The notion of "one true God" is quite appealing by contrast.

You come to silence to find out what you can know when you let your chatter and screens go. The task of silence is to stop doing, to look and to listen. You may hope that after a while you will begin to hear and see in a special way of union with a wider reality which the mystics promise. De Mello says God dances the world.[7] God is in creation as the voice of the singer is in the song. Pay attention to the dance and you may see the dancer. Listen to the song and you may hear the singer, but you must go by the way of opposites. Take time instead of saving time.

Probably 90 percent of the things that upset you cannot be changed. You change what you can and should, and accept what you cannot. De Mello suggests that you list all the elements of your life that you know you can't change, then take each item and say "yes" to it.[8] In learning to say "yes" to all that is, you find peace.

The Outer World

You live connected to everyone and everything. If you would like a quick glimpse of the connection between yourself and the outer world, you might, right this minute, tell a recent story you learned from a newspaper or news broadcast. This is best done in a group because when two or more people tell the same story, you as storyteller shape the story to your own reality. First, one story from among many hooks your attention. Then you tell the story from a certain point of view, omitting some details and emphasizing others. One person's victim drama is another's morality play.

The story you tell, more likely than not, closely relates to something in your own life. For example, one man told the story of an oil tanker with its sleeping crew. The tanker crashed into a ferry full of rollicking holiday celebrants. Treating the story as if it were a personal dream, he identified with each element in turn. He now realized that his workaholic sub-personality was running his life to complete a project at work. It was totally "asleep" to any other considerations. While telling the story, he understood that he had seriously damaged his family's holiday celebrations. He decided that his project could wait. He needed to retrieve his family life.

The different elements of the story represented one person's conflicting drives. There are similar conflicts in groups and ways of helping them. Within limits, the patterns can change. As we do our work of personal integration, the outer groups we work with also change. The ancient Chinese story of the Rain Maker touches this truth. When the people in drought sent for him, the Rain Maker came, selected a small house to dwell in, put it in order, and went about living his ordinary life. After a few days the rains came.

We become "rain makers" as we learn to reverse roles, to enter the point of view of all the different "others" in our lives. As we see and understand, we put our house in order. The rains come, but so softly we scarcely know they have begun.

Stories and Parables

Teachers of all traditions use stories as guides to life change. The best way to use this path is to take a single story, read it over a couple of times, then reflect on it alone or with a study group. Create a silence within you and let the story reveal its inner depth and meaning, something beyond words. Some people find it useful to paint or draw some image from the story but the essential process is to carry the story in your consciousness where it gives fragrance to the events of your day. An example, one of the Sufi stories de Mello uses in his book *Song of the Bird* can serve to close this segment of our work.

> A disciple once complained, "You tell us stories, but you never reveal their meaning to us."
>
> Said the master, "How would you like it if someone offered you fruit and masticated it before giving it to you?"[9]

No one can find your meaning for you. You must eat your own fruit.

Bon appetit!

Chapter Seven:

The Process of Change;
Three Stories

We are all storytellers. We build on each other's insights, and use others' life experiences to comprehend our own. Probably the best preparation for becoming a psychotherapist is an extensive knowledge of literature. The stories, great and small, have all been told. In listening to stories, we come to understand the themes particular to our own lives. Psychotherapists are privileged to act as listeners and to witness the changes that come with understanding. The life stories they listen to are their major source of knowledge.

That is the context for the following three stories. Two are from psychotherapy and one from literature. The first describes change which took place during a five-day period of intensive therapy for an older woman. Her life fitted an Enneagram ONE Program. The second is a look at Dante's journey into his own depths as a paradigm of our own. He progresses through aspects of all Enneagram programs to a unified comprehension of reality transcending ordinary consciousness. The third story details the story of a man in his middle years, sifting the facts of his life, his work and his relationships in an Enneagram FOUR Program.

Martha

Martha's struggle in psychotherapy illustrates that the process of change can begin at any point in the life cycle. She was 67 when she realized she needed help with some of the side effects of her Perfection/Resentment Program. She didn't think of it in those terms, of course. She simply felt "bound up, as though I've never really lived."

Martha's physician referred her for help with a recurrent depression. She saw herself as a victim, being punished without cause. Her periods of depression had begun several years before and occurred only in the fall. Originally, they roughly coincided with Martha's return from vacation to resume charge of a household which included her aged mother and the youngest of her three children, who was still at home.

What about her mother? Why did she live with the family and when had that begun? Martha described her mother with many Enneagram FOUR characteristics—elite standards and difficulty with closeness, but nonetheless a charming woman. She was in good health, financially well provided for at the time of her husband's death. However, that death occurred just as Martha's family was on the verge of moving to Germany on company business, so they invited the mother to join them.

Overseas, Mother was fine with the children and mixed well with the couple's friends, but when invitations did not include her, she was upset and family life became confined to situations which would include her. This made the couple relationship and Martha's separate interests difficult to reconcile. Martha sensed her own anger but swallowed it as inappropriate and unwarranted.

As a ONE, Martha viewed her anger as a fault and avoided expressing it directly. Feelings of any kind are visceral responses which guide us to appropriate action. When we cut ourselves off from a feeling, it is usually because we think the action it requires will put us into intolerable conflict.

We often have to work hard to find appropriate action that is acceptable to all concerned. Recognizing our feelings means not acting on them while the fire is hot but incorporating their direction with our thought and will. Martha's refusal to acknowledge her anger created her impasse. She could not find a solution that would honor and include her own needs for personal freedom and family intimacy. The suppressed feeling of anger grew stronger.

The family returned to the United States. Martha's mother, who had never worked, obtained a job as a companion housekeeper, for her funds were not adequate to cope with inflation. She seemed satisfied. However, shortly before Martha and her husband were to return overseas, her mother suffered a spell of nervous despondency which made it impossible for her to keep the companion job. Again there seemed no alternative but to take her along.

This time after they returned, she was a settled reality in the family's life. She suffered a fall on the ship coming home. Martha described it: "I had to work hard to not spoil the trip for the children. I set my alarm so I could wake in the night and get up to help her to go to the bathroom. Of course, her stateroom was on a different level of the ship." "Of course," I agreed. Martha looked at me defensively: "What are you trying to do? Get me to say I hated my mother? What good would that do? It's all past. She did not intend to be a burden."

Martha heard my challenge correctly. The defense mechanism of the ONE is reaction formation. Martha had reacted in opposition to her anger, burdening herself further. Her difficulty acknowledging personal desires that conflicted with her standards of correctness was apparent in her response to my comment.

Martha's mother lived many years and died in a nursing home. "But I visited her every day even though her mental deterioration kept pace with her physical decline and it seemed so futile."

That was the story on the first of five days of intensive therapy. I gave Martha material to read about the Shadow or dark side of personality. This unpleasant part of us has value which we need to acknowledge but find difficult to accept.

The second day involved teaching her how to relax and enter a light trance state, to allow memories to focus more clearly. She remembered taking her father to the hospital shortly before he died. He spoke to her of the provisions he had made to insure that her mother would be well provided for, since otherwise she could be a burden. "Your mother has always been a spoiled child."

I wondered if Martha remembered telling me that because she was an only child, her mother had made a particular point of not spoiling her, teaching her to behave properly and always do what Mother expected. There seems to have been room for only one spoiled child.

Then I questioned her closely on what happened when the depression came. She described her sleeplessness during the night, her lack of interest in doing anything or being with anyone, her physically weighted, nauseated stomach, her feeling that religion was empty, that her husband was upset and that his care did not reach her. She wished that she might just go to sleep and not wake until Spring.

I checked out that she had not considered suicide, and that she would not. As a registered nurse, Martha was aware of the secondary-gains idea of illness (the "payoff"), so I reminded her of the possibility that at some level, she intended what happened. I wondered if sometimes she wanted to punish her husband for not protecting her from being so overwhelmed by caring for her mother. She rejected this instantly.

Bill had told her to let him take the responsibility of placing her mother in a nursing home when it was clear what this was costing Martha, but "I begged him not to do this. You know what nursing homes are like. She would have died."

I asked, "What finally made it possible to use a nursing home?" Martha's health gave out and her physician said, "It's either you or your mother." She temporized by taking a vacation with a friend. "How did the family manage?" "Mother took care of things while I was gone."(!)

Martha not only denied expression to her resentment but reacted against her feeling by providing an extraordinary level of care. She did not accept her husband's efforts to help her work out other arrangements, nor did she "see" her mother's ability to manage.

On leaving the session, I asked her to work with clay to get a sense of how the depression felt as an entity, then to imagine it alive and capable of speech, and to write a dialogue questioning what it might want of her.

Depression slows us down, and we have to attend to aspects of our lives we may have neglected before it lets us go.

The third day, she resisted the relaxation trance induction. She was restless. Her back hurt. She had expected a miracle and it wasn't happening. The reading did not interest her. She did not want to write and she felt that using art material got her nowhere.

I complimented her strength in resisting what she was not yet ready to accept. She had come to try out new behavior. All her life she had been a "good girl;" she did what others expected. She was right to go on with her own timing. She was ready to use her strength for herself rather than always spending it on others. (This interpretation nonplused her.) We scheduled an additional session.

That afternoon I enacted a psychodrama with her. I had her go back in time to her father's death and become her 40-year-old self deciding to take her 58-year-old mother with the family to Germany. We started with her words, "After all, what else can I do?" I then reversed roles with her and had her play her helpless and depressed mother. Then I asked her again to become her present-age self (67) and we would talk directly to her 58-year-old mother of the past and explore whether she had any options apart from living with her daughter. She had good health, some good friends, and a capacity for managing her own life. I instructed Martha before beginning: "You know what it is like to be fifty-eight. Would you have been that unconscious of what a burden your presence could be to your daughter's family? What advice would you give to your mother from your present age and experience which you did not know at forty?"

Martha had a few pithy comments to make and acknowledged that her mother was not helpless, but she also had some anger at her 40-year-old self for its readiness to take on the martyr role.

Martha and her mother had coped in the best way they knew how at that time, but it was important to know that other feelings and possibilities existed then, because it had something to do with the possibilities now. Her depression was signaling that she could change something in her current life.

In our next session, Martha remembered a dream: Her husband is going to Baltimore. He wants her to join him. There will be only one event for which she will have to dress. She decides to try to get there and finds her way to a rather odd ticket agency which she has to reach in a roundabout way, down some stairs, and up again. The woman in the agency says she can arrange the trip, but Martha will have to find out the exact distance and then they will decide the cost. Martha must put up a bond that she will pay if she wishes to go. While she is trying to figure out how she can supply the right information, another woman appears and says she has a computer and can figure this out for her. Yes, she decides, she can and will pay the cost.

The ticket office was Martha's metaphor for the intensive psychotherapy experience. She had to decide her goal and if she was willing to pay the cost. When locating the right information baffled her, another feminine unknown part of her supplied the answer.

On the day of our last session the final World Series game was being played in Baltimore. Martha identified her dream's use of that site as a metaphor for her goal. It was where the action was—where life was.

Her husband was already there waiting for her. Her recognition of the hopefulness and the meaning of this dream brought tears to our eyes.

She was now ready to know and own her Shadow qualities. All her life, Martha had followed her mother's directives. She did what others expected, did not give in to herself, and was not spoiled. Nor did she let herself be given much. Her Shadow or unlived side contained her repressed anger and manipulative self-will, but it also contained her playful creativity, her unorthodox, independent imagination and a looser, freer relation to her body. She had never let herself fully enjoy her husband's zest and her own sexuality.

Martha had never let herself be openly angry with him either, so she half-consciously insured he would be made uncomfortable in other ways when he displeased her. She had so little connection to the free-child aspect of her personality that it, like a neglected child, was demanding that she hear and acknowledge it.

She found it difficult to see the depression as the ugly side of this neglected child within and to believe that it would lighten as she allowed herself to receive what her husband wanted to give. She had to decide that she wanted to live her full life. Her anger at her mother's unconscious extortion had been hidden by a world model in which love and anger could not co-exist. This also made her marriage difficult.

Her guilt for the anger conflicted with her own need for love and allowed only the negative attention gained by her depression.

Old ways of pain are the familiar habits of addiction. New growth is always disturbing. It didn't feel like the miracle she wanted, but her dreams knew. Shortly before she left, she had a dream that it was Christmas and children were about to open doors.

Dante—An Example From Literature

Perhaps the greatest classic of Western literature describing the mid-life crisis—the question of what we are doing here, the consequences of our choices (particularly the narrow, self-centered ones), and the steps of transformation of consciousness—is Dante's *Divine Comedy*. A contemporary person hardly expects a 14th century epic, particularly one that deals with "hell," to be relevant to his or her concerns.

However, Dante captures our interest beginning with the image of a man waking up in a dark woods, in which at midlife he has lost his way. This seems a perfect metaphor for the state when familiar goals (power, family respectability, success, rebellion, social reform, whatever used to matter) seem empty and pointless: that state which one man characterized as "no debts, a clear mortgage, retirement plans—BIG DEAL—and it's all absurd."

As we read Dante and his commentators, we begin to see that the Inferno, Purgatory and Paradise correspond to three "here and now" states of consciousness familiar to us all. Dante stumbles about, as we do, until he finds a guide. We find guidance only when we realize we need help. Virgil, Dante's guide, symbolizes reason and human discipline.

As with Martha, finding the way involves going down into unpleasant self-knowledge. Virgil takes Dante down into the Inferno and then on to the mountain of Purgatory. The Shadow addictions of the Enneagram correspond to the stages in the Inferno and these qualities again appear in their transformation on the levels of the Mountain.

William Soskin, in a paper comparing *The Divine Comedy* to *The Tibetan Book of the Dead*, the shaman's journey and other death-rebirth processes opening self-knowledge, describes the "mortal sins" of the Inferno as errors of perception and decision-making—grave errors, which cause serious distortion and poor choices, which in turn further determine persistent misperception.

> Sin is an error-generating process. Catharsis, whether through therapy or through confession, causes an erasing of the board that allows us to see reality in a new light.[1]

Dante reveals his own weaknesses with ruthless honesty as he travels downward. His understanding of the deepening dangers of ego-centricity expresses itself in the order of his descent. He finds people just inside the gate of Hell who continue self-pitying, futile fence-sitting—just as we do when we know what must be done but keep counting the cost. The inadequate and self-indulgent follow on the other side of a thin line which we do not want to recognize when we cross it: the line between desire and lust, between enjoyment of good things and greed, between spontaneous anger and half-conscious cruelty.[2]

He uses three transition points to mark the deepening alienation of the Inferno state of consciousness. The first is entry into the violent city of Dis, the second is the passage into fraud, and the final passage is the pit in the icy depths of ultimate evil, the cannibalism of betrayal of the inner meaning and very roots of love.

Dante uses his images to evoke awareness that "sin," the egocentric choice, creates and maintains its own specific impasse and stuckness. Martha's distorted denial of her anger imprisoned her. Contrary to the popular idea, there are no punishments in either the Inferno or Purgatory. Every act or attitude, insofar as it does not come from the wholeness beyond the narrow interests of the ego, carries within itself its own penalty.

Penalty means payment of a debt. Eastern thought defines it in the doctrine of Karma. Dante uses his extraordinary images of suffering for the same purpose. Heavy millstones and rich garments imprison those who placed their importance in how they appeared to other men (the THREE strategy of Achievement and Image). A cold wind blows ceaselessly, tossing about those who lusted and misused passion for their ego-centric purposes (the EIGHT strategy of Self-defined Justice with Arrogance): cold, because lust, unlike the heat of genuine desire, is ultimately cold and abusive.

The different images mirror our reality, but owning the projected Shadow is not easy. Recognition begins the process of transformation. Dante has to deal with his own particular problems of lust and pride. He emerges from the dark pit of the Inferno, with its black confusion and meaningless suffocation, just before dawn. Before him open the clean, sapphire-blue darkness and the brilliant stars of the Southern Cross. This image conveys the turning point when darkness lightens. We leave the pain of the Inferno in only one way—by accepting another type of suffering which is purging.

That suffering comes with the search for meaning and the acceptance of responsibility for the life we have created. Dante conveys this in his description of climbing the Mountain of Purgatory, which he has located in the southern hemisphere, the other side of the world.

His definition of his tasks suggests an Enneagram position between EIGHT and TWO; however, the evidence in his work of extraordinary comprehension of all known fields of knowledge suggests a place between FIVE and SEVEN, while his pursuit of perfection in the composition of the 100 Cantos, and the clear pleasure he takes in placing his enemies in the Inferno, point to aspects of Enneagram ONE. His early life loss of Beatrice and the transformation of this loss and longing into the images of the Paradiso have the flavor of the FOUR Program. What Dante achieves in his work is a synthesis of all the human life tasks.

The Purgatory of Dante's vision is not an outmoded doctrine of the Church. Every person who chooses the way of consciousness lives it in the tension of opposing drives and feelings. The mountain Dante climbs is primarily a place to learn contemplation.

Contemplation is an attitude toward life. It implies the ability to look at and reflect on what we see with feeling as well as thought, involvement as well as detachment. In Purgatory all sins can now be seen not only as errors in perception, but as active distortions of the forms of love. We can correct them.

Pride (Enneagram Shadow of point TWO), Envy (point FOUR) and Wrath (point ONE) need to be transformed into Humility, Contentment and Forbearance. They are errors of ego-centric love. Sloth is inadequate love (point NINE). We exercise possessive love when we fail to apply our capacity to love appropriately for the good of all rather than the maximum use of one in Avarice (point FIVE), Gluttony (point SEVEN) and Lust (point EIGHT). The Cowardice of Enneagram point SIX has already been implicitly transformed into the courageous love necessary to make the journey.

After passing through the earthly garden of Paradise and the waters of forgetting and remembering, Dante progressively learns to surrender to the modes of loving experience. He can no longer depend on reason, but his puzzled questioning of the paradoxes of human existence continues. He has entered a new dimension in this model of reality (the realm of mystical experience described in all spiritual traditions, East and West).

The ordinary ideas of time and space no longer apply. He uses the metaphor of ascending through the planets, sun and stars, but he tells us from the beginning that the state of bliss is one. All souls dwell equally at the center, a description evocative of the poet Eliot's "at the still point, there the dance/is," and the physicist Einstein's description of the center of the universe as a point which is everywhere.[3]

In ordinary consciousness, our minds cannot grasp unity which contains all diversity and is beyond time and space. Yet the sense of this model is not so different from the contemporary thought of Jung and Teilhard de Chardin, that the more distinct from others you become, the closer you are to the All.

The goal of individuation is individual completeness, not perfection. The people Dante meets in Paradise are all fulfilled. They differ

Enneagram Programs

Shadow Issue	Program	Strength
1. Wrath	Perfection with resentment	forbearance, serenity
2. Pride	Service with manipulation	humility
3. Deceit	Efficiency with emphasis on image	truth, hope
4. Envy	Excellence with melancholic nostalgia	contentment
5. Avarice	Knowledge with withdrawal and stinginess	detachment
6. Cowardice	Security with fear and doubt	courage, faith
7. Gluttony	Easy Idealism with multiple plans and options	temperance
8. Lust	Self-defined Justice with vengeance	innocence
9. Indolence	Non-aggression with indecision and indolence	action, love

The Shadow issue names are those of the traditional Deadly Sins. For psychological purposes we can view these in the terms Soskin did above, as errors of perception and decision-making which cause distortion and bad choices resulting in continued misperception. We look for an objective view of reality. The strengths are gained in wrestling with the Shadow issue specific to each program.

only in the ways they have kept themselves from experiencing the ultimate.

This thought, that the only thing that you are called to become is the individual that only you can be, places profound worth on each of us.

Dante's model of reality was rooted in medieval understandings, but he was an extraordinarily close observer of human behavior and the physical facts of his world. He offers a vision of the totality of reality which challenges us to be as comprehensive.

Max

The complexity of grappling with one's personal Shadow and distinguishing its particular character can be illustrated with the life story of a man following an Enneagram FOUR Program of high standards. His relationship with his wife (who was in an Enneagram SEVEN strategy of multiple plans and avoidance of pain) frustrated him and forced him to grow.

Max, a musician and poet from Argentina, came to this country in the fifties. As a classicist poet, he had little interest in the literature of the "beat generation," so he undertook new studies. He chose engineering as the quickest way to gain professional recognition and to provide a lifestyle comparable to his family background. He poured himself into his studies. When he graduated, he was known as a perfectionist with a complex and intricate mind. He described this period later: "I seemed to have my future well in hand, but then, as usual, I made a fatal mistake." The mistake, he felt, was his marriage. The woman he chose, vivacious and attractive, came from a professional family background, although no one in her family seemed to have accomplished much.

Initially, this did not disturb him, and as they started a family of their own, he devoted much of his time and thought to designing and building their home. He took every detail into consideration, not only architectural details but also the plumbing, electricity, geology and the selection of native plants that would hold the land and complement his design. None of this particularly interested his wife. As he thought about it later, she did not seem aware, much less appreciative, of his work. She professed not to understand anything mechanical and laughed, saying that when she came near machines, bad things happened, e.g., she accidentally damaged his tools or erased musical tapes he valued. She often complained that he was too tired from all this work to do things with her and the children. So the years went by and he withdrew more and more into his work.

Now in her early forties, Max's wife considered applying to graduate school or possibly taking a job, as the children were adolescent and no longer needed her as they had earlier. She joined a midlife planning group where her personal warmth and empathetic feelings made her well liked by other women.

She soon concluded that her marriage was not happy. She experienced her husband as constantly depressed and irritable at home. She had learned not to take seriously his morbid introspection about his health and probable early death, but the influence of his pessimism on their children bothered her. They (and she) felt they could not live up to his expectations. She wanted them to know they were lovable and did not have to achieve anything to be worthwhile.

She had been in love with Max when they married, but during the birth of their children it became clear to her that he did not love her in the same way. Both times he had arranged to be away on field trips. She admired his knowledge and pleasure in music and wanted him to share this with her, but she was frightened to touch his precious records when he was not there. She had little insight into her anger toward her husband or anything she might be contributing to make the marriage difficult. Following the group discussion, however, she was sufficiently troubled to share her concern with Max about his depressed moods and to urge him to seek help.

Max came readily to therapy. He recognized that he was suffering from depression and said it had been chronic throughout his life. Recently it had gotten so bad, he feared he might take his life, for he knew he could not go on living like this. He spoke of his mother's warning when he was a child: "We are not a lucky family. Do not expect your dreams to come true." He added, "She spoke the truth. Nothing has ever worked out for me." He knew his colleagues respected him, but somehow success always eluded him. He felt that his mother was right. He had success within his hand and he could not grasp it.

He spoke with bitterness of the long hours of hard work he had put into the early home before his wife decided it was too isolating and moved them into a tract house in a community she preferred. In disbelief at her stupidity, he put up no protest. If she could not see, he could not open her eyes. What did it matter anyway? He would be dead in a few years, if not sooner.

As sessions continued, Max's story unfolded. An oldest son and his mother's favorite, he identified more with her values and point of view than with his father's. A capable woman with more intelligence and ability than anyone else he knew, she had talents that could not flower "in the wrong time and the wrong place."

Max's depression lifted as he told his story, read extensively in this new field of interest, and expressed his feelings. Some hitherto unknown aspects of his life had come to light. He was not only respected but also well liked by almost everyone as warm, witty and generous in working with other people's problems. In followup sessions with his wife, however, his implacable anger, and her corresponding cruelty which discounted what he had provided for the family and sabotaged his efforts and interests, made it clear that the marriage was at an impasse which neither willed to break. They both agreed the marriage was over.

Several years later, Max returned to therapy. He feared he might be sinking into an immobilizing depression similar to the one he had come through. He had recently put together a process to extract oil from shale. This time he had lined up a business partner he felt he could trust. He had important appointments scheduled throughout the coming month but his depression made it all seem like dust. He knew he was going to throw in the towel, as he had before.

He talked about the marriage. He said that his wife had hired a vicious attorney. Max assented to their demands without a fight. She was "an idiot, a parasite, congenitally incapable of earning her own way." Of course, he would support her. He bitterly resented the lawyer and methods she chose, but he did not hire a lawyer to defend his interests. He had nothing but contempt for the breed. So, she had the house with the pool, all their assets and an alimony of half his income until the children left college. He, who had worked so hard, had nothing but his business and ability to earn a living.

At this point we can return to the theory of the Shadow and describe its development. Max grew up closely identified with his talented mother who saw her abilities mirrored in him and nourished them. However, from her own experience, she passed on another legacy, her Enneagram FOUR strategy and mindset—the family was "unlucky." He could not count on his dreams being realized. He would work hard but not be successful.

His ego consciously identified with his intellect, curiosity and capacity for hard work. He could develop his abilities (to please others) so long as his enjoyment of them remained unconscious. His spontaneous, childlike lightheartedness and irresponsible feeling side were similarly repressed as "not us." Depression and resentment were "familiar," and as such, assimilated by his ego. Acting on his anger to protect his self-interest and self-esteem was not acceptable and was repressed. His father did not provide a sufficiently strong counter to his mother's perspective. When he married, he sought the missing elements for wholeness in his wife, not a bad choice from this point of view. However, the FOUR difficulty with intimacy surfaced, focusing his attention on the negative aspects of what he had. His mother had a similar elitist contempt for her mate.

Max's FOUR-ONE Enneagram strategy axis contributes a further explanation by looking at his ego's driving emphasis on detail and perfection and his unfulfilled expectation that his wife would appreciate and admire his work. His wife had hooks for all that he repressed in himself and found unacceptable: her careless acceptance of imperfection, lighthearted lack of self-discipline and her marked ego-centricity. Note his rancorous words, however: "idiot," "parasite," "congenitally incapable of supporting herself." Projecting a bit of one's Shadow incites this style of speech. The polarization was too extreme, not complementary, and integration had clearly not occurred. At this time, both partners refused the opportunity this interpersonal dispute/depression offered to grapple with their own and each other's Shadow qualities. They refused to make the relationship yield its treasure. Both operated from dependency hungers that neither would acknowledge.

Notice the similar use of the husband's workaholism, an addiction to work, and its apparent opposite, the wife's laziness. They both provide an escape from relationship. Addicts of various kinds (alcoholics, overeaters, drug abusers) implicitly act as if they expect help to arrive from outside to take care of them. Change, however, is only possible when they decide to act on their own behalf. Workaholism, in contrast to other addictions, gains society's approval, false nourishment substituted for genuine relationship. It thus reinforces the depressive's refusal to change, refusal to engage with the substance and relationships of his personal life. In Enneagram terms, as a FOUR, Max was attracted to his wife's SEVEN attributes: her playfulness, idealism, social skills, self-centered charm and appetite for life. He needed similar qualities in himself to relieve his melancholic stance and isolation. After he married her, however, his view shifted. He saw the same attributes as superficial, irresponsible, greedy and narcissistic. In turn, he did not take in her information about his own Shadow qualities of envy, elitism and addiction to melancholy.

One sees one's partner's Shadow more clearly than that of anyone else, but strongly resists taking the information and recognizing one's own projections.

Max had to experience much pain before he could come to recognize his own inertia at critical moments as a refusal to know his hunger and deal with his fear. When he did so, he was able to integrate his personal and professional life on a new basis.

His wife, having secured all the couple's assets as her own, still did not recognize that the "materialistic greed" she projected onto him was her own, a substitute for her hunger to be loved. She refused to risk giving back. In so doing, she crossed from "futile self-pity to self-indulgence, from enjoyment of good things to greed, from anger to cruelty." Nevertheless, in moving down into her own dark aspects, she began to wake to her individual values, and her own journey of consciousness began.

Projections differ from common errors of perception in that the person denies them with passion and cannot be convinced. "Louder and wronger" is the usual defense. Sooner or later, however, the projection weakens. This is not seen as such, but one experiences a sense of listless despondency or dispiritedness. Energy drains off into the unconscious complex which is pushing to be known. With time, this emerges first in dreams, then in consciousness itself.

Max's ability, strength and intellectual ingenuity made success inevitable in a receptive culture. His mother's legacy message contained one error; her pattern did not apply to her son. He was in a highly suitable field, the talented son of a cherishing mother, not a daughter born at the turn of the century into macho Latin American culture. His Shadow contained much of his spontaneity, the raw energy of his self-interest to act, and the unacceptable indolence which he needed to know in order to bring leisure, pleasure and balance into his life.

In many lifelong depressions, beneath the crippling stagnation of the personality there is some sort of intense desire (for power, love, expansion, aggression) which the depressed person does not dare allow to come to the surface. Von Franz compares this to the fabled fox who finds the grapes too sour.

Success threatened Max. It meant that his repressed feelings, his desire for success and self-assertive aggression were breaking through. He had to face down the fear, the other side of his desire, and engage with someone and something to make it happen. He had to stop withdrawing, running away and hiding at critical moments. He had to know his intense passionate wanting and allow its possibility. Paradoxically, he also had to dis-identify with his work's success by accepting the possibility of its failure.

He had to stop isolating himself and be willing to engage in the give and take of ordinary peer friendships and conflicts. He had to let himself and others know his warts: that he had an irascible temper and had to struggle with his arrogance, that he no longer wanted, much less needed, to take care of everyone's needs while losing sight of his own. He had to give up his isolated, romantic self-definition as victim.

He had to know his own anger at having accepted his mother's inauthentic definition of life for so many years. He had to accept the words of Conrad's character Stein in *Lord Jim*: "To survive...to the destructive element submit yourself, and with the exertion of your hands and feet in the water make the deep, deep sea keep you up."[4] Max had to look at himself as he was. He had to face the truth.

Chapter Eight:

Peacemaking, Integration and Laughter

You have no choice. You must place your bet.—Pascal

We are in the crack of change between two ages. Once we cross the threshold, our experience of the world will shift dramatically, as it did in the Industrial Revolution and the Renaissance.

We have almost instantaneous communication everywhere. The microelectronic revolution has transformed information media. The last thirty years have brought momentous changes to our understanding of the human mind; feminism has shifted awareness to different levels of life; "liberation" movements have swept through groups and nations; and Third World countries are challenging conventional economics. New alliances, such as Amnesty International, and coalitions, such as the anti-pesticide network, are linking individuals and groups in ways that are non-bureaucratic and nonviolent, working to heal the pangs of transition.

However, as a society we have specific threshold problems with no clear solutions; the Enneagram programs of anger, fear and repression are world as well as individual issues. For the most part, we are still responding in old Enneagram forms of fight, flight and submission. The technology is new, but the Shadow forces of narcissistic arrogance, greed and the like still lurk in the structures of power, East and West, North and South.

It is tempting to see these problems as black and white, and insoluble. The pollution of our air, water and soil now reflects the destruction we have brought to other species. As we face the proliferation of countries capable of starting nuclear war, a formidable task is to contain our destructive urges long enough so that the world survives. Yet military power continues to be the preferred means to settle disputes between—and within—nations.[1] At the community level, the abuse of drugs and alcohol by ever-younger children, the physical and sexual abuse of children, the gang-war killings among teenagers, the numerous forms of addiction and the demoralization of homeless families are but a few signs of our distress. Each promotes darker, heavier Enneagram programming.

Many people view their world as intolerable. A contemporary ethical principle, called the intuition of justice, states that a society is just if individuals, not knowing what their place in that society would be, can accept it as just.[2] To test it, let's assume that we have yet to be born into this world and that we do not know into which country, class, race or family we will be born. A tiny elite controls and consumes most of the world's goods and services, and the vast majority is poor. We're probably going to be born into that impoverished majority. Now answer the question: Is this a just society? From this exercise you can see that as people come to consciousness, they are not going to accept the system as it stands.

In some sense, whole societies must therefore die and be reborn. Steven Kull, a psychologist studying our attraction to war and the irrational nature of the nuclear arms race, postulates that there is an unconscious attraction to world destruction and death. But destruction implies the possibility of transformation (death/rebirth).[3] Evidence of this can be found in those who attempt suicide. The difference between those who recover and those who try again is that the people who recover make a major life change. They are no longer the same people. They were actually seeking the death of an intolerable self-image or world image. This is exactly what we have been wrestling with in our Enneagram shifts.

If humankind is to survive, we must comprehend how powerful our destructive impulses are—our rage, our boredom and our hunger for a life that makes sense. We need to collectively relate to these Shadow urges in a different way.

The inner world of each of us mirrors the outer world we live in. Millions of us are experimenting with the same forces and the same questions. We encounter the opposites in our sexuality. We try to find and use different forms of power. We try to find ways of relating to what seems intolerable and unacceptable. Step by step, we are creating the climate for a radical shift in collective consciousness necessary to deal with this changing world.

Reframing is the essence of our human tactic for dealing with threat. It is the artful, human alternative to fighting, fleeing or submitting. It allows us to be more inclusive in our perception, and it begins at the individual level.

Humor and Reframing

One wonderful human asset in our struggle for transformation is humor. Two hundred years ago, Goethe, in an episode of suicidal despair, tried several times to stab himself through the heart. He couldn't run the knife through his clothing, which finally struck him as funny. When he laughed, he gave up his suicidal attempts and turned his attention to writing. A sense of humor doesn't mix well with self-destruction.

Laughter makes survival possible. When we use it to defuse potentially dangerous situations, it's an unbeatable alternative to violence. Humor substitutes intellectual aggression, wit, satire, caricature and irony for bloodshed and destruction; it is also intellectually creative. In the moment we break the set of our perceptions and reframe an event, we share a more objective point of view with the other people involved.

For example, James Farmer, organizing boycotts and sit-ins, told the story of a black man ordered to the back of the bus. The man rose to his feet and answered softly: "Sir, you have just made two mistakes. I am not a 'boy,' and I am not one of them non-violent Negroes." Farmer, a black man talking to blacks in a non-violent context, recognized and could touch the opposite feelings in them. When we laugh at ourselves, healing and health begin; when we can laugh with others at a frightening or painful reality, we bond together to get through difficult times.

Personal Integration and the Collective

Our choices always affect others. We can't take on all of society's problems, but we can start with those to which we are directly connected or which move us emotionally. If we can envision the way things would be if a given problem or conflict did not exist, the best "win-win" outcome, then we can work backwards and arrive at the steps we must take to reach that state. In other words, we see what should have changed immediately beforehand and, in turn, what changes would be required before that step.

Take an example from family therapy: If a parent is to stop physically abusing a child and the family is to remain together, the child has to be physically protected. The parent has to feel less tension in order to be able to create a safer and more cherishing climate. Each of these conditions has its own preconditions. Who protects the child? When? How? Dealing with the parents' threshold of violence may first require helping one of them locate work to develop a sense of self-esteem. A more cherishing climate involves all members of the family and portions of the problem have to be tackled on a community level. We have to provide either adequate, safe childcare or support a family wage that allows a parent to provide care in person.

In this type of analysis we can work back to find the first step that is feasible and possible for us, as individuals, to take. The work of integration happens first within individuals. Each personal choice to encounter the Shadow's destructive force aids the collective choice. In a time when "individualism" has so many negative connotations, it is difficult to believe in the individual and trust this process, but the choice of consciousness exists only here. As we each work on our Enneagram Program, we learn to deal realistically with opposite points of view in the wider society.

As Lily Tomlin's baglady Trudy puts it, "After all, what is reality anyway? Nothin' but a collective hunch....a primitive method of crowd control..."[4] So, let us play the hand we were dealt, and place our bets. It's our only choice.

Appendix:

The Individual as a Microcosm of What Is Going On in the World
(A Jungian Slant on General Systems Theory)

In psychology, as in every other profession and discipline, our attention has shifted from "what" to "how." We emphasize the process of integration within the individual, the processes of relationship—how conflicts develop and how to resolve them. We are moving from defining people in categories to recognizing that we can describe their behavior as energy organized in fixed patterns. Within limits, the patterns can change.

An initial pattern, or strategy, like the first mark on a blank piece of paper, sets up what can follow, but life continues to present issues that we can't handle easily within a set program. Probably each of us faces some version of all the Enneagram tasks during a lifetime.

My thesis is that *the individual is a microcosm of what is going on in the outer world. The inner world of each of us mirrors the outer world we live in.*

Some Jungian Concepts of the Inner and Outer Worlds

Before we consider our collective problems, some Jungian definitions and a description of the net of their relationships may be useful:

The *ego* is the center of the conscious personality. While you think of it simply as "I" or "myself," it includes a complex of activities. You will, you choose, and you remember. You learn to comply with the demands of your parents and your culture in childhood. Your ego includes collective cultural and moral values as well as your Enneagram strategy for survival.

As your ego develops, a rift occurs within. You have to deal with feelings, attitudes and thoughts that do not fit the laws and regulations around you. "Disobedience" mixes with self-disgust, anxiety and feelings of guilt—but also potential self-reliance. You learn to suppress, and sometimes entirely repress from your consciousness, the painful conflicts of your opposing feelings and thoughts. This process develops what Jungians call the *personal Shadow.*

The *Self,* the center of your total personality, is also a dynamic process. It potentially includes your ego, your personal unconscious and, like a hologram, everything of which you are or can become conscious. It is a potential state of wholeness and inclusion.

As with the wave and the particle theories of light, images of the Self can help us understand aspects, but they do not explain its full reality. Take another metaphor. In some sense, the Self is like a water well. At its deepest level it taps into an underlying water table from which all other wells also draw their life. When we say we want to feel centered, we mean we want to feel the connection between our ego and Self, and through this Self the connection to all selves and all that is.

An inner urge coming from the Self seems to push us to forge a unified personality. It grows stronger as we respond to our life tasks. One of the great things about the human life cycle is that if we don't "get the message" the first time around, the issues turn up over and over until we finally do.

When we make the choice to work at unifying our personalities, the parts we repressed return to confront us. We mature when we include these thoughts and feelings in our sense of self. But integration cannot take place unless we both admit these tendencies and allow them some measure of realization. The ability to oppose must be real if ethics are to make any sense. It's basic to choice and self-reliance. For example, our honesty is only tested in the temptation to lie; our commitment, in the temptation to infidelity. We learn our limits and know our choices.

The personal Shadow takes a different form in each Enneagram program. It seems repugnant and unacceptable and, when alienated, it can invade our behavior in evil ways. To admit "I don't know what possessed me" can be the first step in Shadow recognition. Accepting the problem of the Shadow does not imply identification with evil or an inflated notion of being beyond good and evil. Acknowledging your dark aspect means that you are no longer unconscious of the problem and no longer can project or deny it.

Encounter with some form of evil (pain, loss of meaning, something that appears destructive) seems to be necessary to start us on the path to consciousness. We burn away our own weakness and gain strength only through conflict with what opposes wholeness and inclusion. Often we struggle with a blank sense of impasse. The task is to choose to endure the tension of opposites ("I can't and yet I must"). Then some quite small shift occurs. Out of this small, suddenly noticeable difference comes a wider consciousness.

We might define evil in the *collective Shadow* as whatever opposes life or kills any aspect of a sense of choice (awareness, mobility, growth, autonomy, will). Measures to control people, discouraging their capacity to think for themselves, to diminish their unpredictability, robbing them of their humanity—these are evil.

Paradoxically, evil is a necessity for the development of a sense of self to occur, but its presence does not guarantee it will take place. Too often, as happened in the Nazi SS or more recently the death squads of Central America, the person's moral fiber erodes upon exposure to evil. Accepting the reality of evil is necessary, but complacency toward it is dangerous.

The Shadow is not evil. When it is made conscious, recognized and owned, it brings new energy, strength and direction to our life. Our consciousness can enlarge to include forgiveness and healing. But before the gifts comes the struggle. This wholeness, which comes about through imperfection, requires a descent into the dangerous realm of the unconscious. The stories of Chapter Seven illustrate this, as Martha struggled with her destructive anger, and Max had to deal with his competitive envy.

The *collective unconscious* appears at first to be the sum of the patterns of experience found in all human beings. Beneath these structures and strategies, however, we find a deeper unity. We need openness and caring to bring its creative content over the threshold into consciousness. The Enneagram offers a net to gather the connections.

Individuation is the process of meeting the unconscious and transforming and integrating our inner oppositions. This process allows the self to emerge in us as individual human beings. As we each become our unique selves, we connect more deeply to specific people, then to all humanity. We each gather around us what might be thought of as our own "soul family," a group of people not created by accident, but rather through a deeper, more essential spiritual interest or concern: reciprocal individuation. Marie-Louise von Franz describes this type of relationship as having something strictly objective, strangely transpersonal about it, with a sense of immediate, timeless "being-together."[1]

There is a communal aspect to our identity. As we strive for individuation, we build on each other's thoughts and insights, and struggle toward a collective consciousness. This appears in groups and in families. Family therapists see an identified patient (the one others regard as "crazy" or delinquent) as acting out the Shadow side of a family group. We intervene to help the family recognize the child's values, even though the child is expressing them in a negative way. We help the family find ways to include the child's perspective. As the family does so, the conflicts are resolved. The family unifies itself with a stronger sense of identity.

Similarly, in community crises, when we take time to enter the mindset of the individual(s) concerned, we often can heal the irruption of Shadow violence. The stress has come from needs the group has refused to deal with. Many "us vs. them" polarizations need a process to include and transform them. Members participate in and influence the community's conscious and unconscious aspects.

Some Notes From Systems Theory

Groups often behave with patterns similar to those a person uses. We have been considering family and the community conflicts that are similar to the conflict of ego and Shadow within the individual. Each can be solved by a process which includes everyone's needs. So we will now look at ways in which the person is like the group and the group like the larger community, using a general systems theory. We will attend to the Shadow element which needs to be included.

Donald T. Brown defines a system as an organization of interacting parts with a boundary.[2] The community, the group and the person each have a boundary. The person's heart has a boundary; an individual cell in the heart also has a boundary. Each of these entities is a living system.

Living systems stay alive by taking in matter and energy through their boundaries. They can accumulate excess, grow and develop. A child obviously grows, but so does a group, in a different way.

Growth moves in steps of stability, then change to greater complexity, then stability again. The system itself governs these shifts. For example, adolescents grow awkwardly in spurts of growth, then periods of stability during which they physically coordinate. Similarly, a group can be thought of as growing in spurts. It experiences conflict, then needs a period of time to identify and integrate what it has learned. It can then experiment in using the learning. We identify group developmental tasks and sequences.

We can examine a group as a living system from several points of view. Actions may be totally explained from each perspective. Which one we choose affects what we see that we can do. We can take the point of view of the whole group; or that of the roles played by the different factions; or that of the recurring interactions between members; or, finally, the point of view of the individual.

For example, in geopolitical struggles we can probe the meaning of religious fundamentalism gaining power in places as different as the Middle East, Latin America and the United States. When we take the point of view of the whole, we ask, "What are the people of the late twentieth century Earth concerned with, that this is taking place? What is valuable or useful in what is happening? What structures are trying to emerge?" (For example, in the American colonies' struggle over "states' rights," a federal government structure was pushing to birth.)

Groups change as a result of actions which are at first insignificant. An intervention which may seem puny (for instance, to study the evolving system) actually feeds back into the system, and wider group support can develop to identify useful change initiatives.

Another point of view focuses on group roles: We explain behavior as a group phenomenon. The group reacts to its awareness of universal human feelings (trust, aggression, loss) or conflicts (dependency, destructiveness), and a member or subgroup emerges as a container for a wished for, or feared, reaction. In our example of religious fundamentalism, focusing on the group role point of view directs our attention to the specific groups who contain the fundamentalists. We notice that each group is also reacting aggressively to some assumed or real threat to its self-determination (loss of land and resources). Furthermore, the degree of violence and "irrationality" has some relation to the degree of deprivation. The question to ask is: "What issues, of concern to all the group member nations, do these nations embody?" Self-determination in relation to a modern world economy is one aspect. What appeared to be Shadow aggression now appears to embody a needed point of view, no matter how difficult it may be to address.

That different groups are in different stages of development complicates our analysis. Interventions, to whatever extent they are possible, have to address these issues at the level of nations or powerful international organizations.

We can see behavior in groups with smaller boundaries in terms of roles. The United States Congress with its political factions sometimes exhibits behavior resembling the choreographed movements of a dance. Matters of strong conflict call forth action and equally powerful steps of inaction. Consider the function of the Senate filibuster. Although a Shadow tactic, it can serve a valuable role for political minority groups, as idealized in the film *Mr. Smith Goes to Washington.*

Group role interventions include anything which helps the group take responsibility for what it projects in situations of fear and prejudice.

The point of view of one group member differs from the rest. For example, the senator who conducts a filibuster is acting in a role, but he may also have a personal affinity for playing the rebel. At this level, his behavior is explained in terms of recurring patterns of interaction with his colleagues. Attempts to change his behavior include anything which calls attention to these patterns. Comments from the media sometimes serve this function.

The personal point of view, yet another level, explains individual behavior according to whatever theory (frame of reference) is chosen, including that of the Enneagram.

The Work of Integration

The task at each level is to bring the oppositions into relationship. Giving each side its own dignity is a necessary precondition. Healing the effects of the personal or collective Shadow is only possible when we are willing to look at it directly and agree to the encounter.

Systems theory is a powerful tool, but there are many approaches to healing and many sources of knowledge. The great myths of humankind hold the notion of our oneness, the interconnection of all humanity. They also describe in remarkable metaphors the developmental steps for individual and group integration. There are problems in realizing this in a practical way. De-speciation is an example—"We're humans, but you're not."

What a fully human and integrated world would look like is not yet clear to us. It seems to be a goal of our long journey.

Accepting the proposition that the individual's inner world is a microcosm of the outer world, we are left with questions: Can we, individually, let ourselves recognize and own the Shadow side, the "acting-out" behavior of our community groups and our political/economic systems? Can we acknowledge the degree of our ability to develop the means of wholeness and inclusion? And can we each find the small steps that begin to gather our separate visions and know them as one?

Notes

Acknowledgements

1. Carl G. Jung, *The Structure and Dynamics of the Psyche* (New York: Pantheon Books, 1960), p.307.

Preface

1. Cf. Lawrence Fine, "Kabbalistic Texts" Chapter Six, Barry W. Holtz (ed.), *Back to the Sources: Reading the Classic Jewish Texts* (New York: Simon & Schuster, 1984), pp. 305-359.

2. P.D. Ouspensky, *In Search of the Miraculous* (San Diego: Harcourt Brace Jovanovich, 1949), p. 294.

3. Charles Tart, *Transpersonal Psychologies* (New York: Harper and Row, 1975), p. 329.

4. *Diagnostic and Statistical Manual of Mental Disorders: DSM-III-R* (Washington, D.C.: American Psychiatric Association, 1987).

Part I: Introduction

1. This clinical usage is to be distinguished from conventional Enneagram terminology of Head, Heart and Belly Centers, and the Palmer paradigm of Anger, Fear and Hysteria.

2. P.D. Ouspensky, ibid., p.289.

Chapter One

1. A set of tapes, *Liars and Lying*, originally published by the University of California, 1974, is currently available directly from Dr. Carl Faber in Santa Monica, California and is useful in treatment of this disorder.

2. Carl G. Jung, *Psychology and Alchemy* (Princeton, N.J.: Princeton University Press, 1968), p. 230.

3. Theodore Roethke, "In a Dark Time" in *Collected Poems* (New York: Doubleday, 1966), p. 239.

Chapter Two

1. T.S. Eliot, "East Coker" in *Four Quartets* (San Diego: Harcourt Brace Jovanovich, 1971), p. 29.

2. "The fear of the Lord is the beginning of wisdom": Psalm 111, line 10.

3. Data from the National Crime Survey, 1975-1984, indicate that one out of every 30 black men will become a murder victim. (U.S. Department of Justice, Bureau of Justice Statistics, technical report, GPO 1987 181-478:40027, p. 1)

4. Theodore Millon, *Disorders of Personality* (New York: John Wiley, 1981), pp. 167-8.

Chapter Three

1. John Enright, "On the Playing Fields of Synanon" in *Confrontation: Encounters in Self and Impersonal Awareness*, Blank, Gottesegan and Gottesegan, editors (New York: Macmillan, 1970), p. 161.

2. It is still not clear why such a widely respected therapeutic community went wrong, but its decay is described in William F. Olin's *Escape From Utopia* (Santa Cruz, California: Peace Press, 1980).

3. The Bible (RSV), Sam. 12, 1-7.

4. Peter Berger, *The Precarious Vision* (New York: Doubleday, 1961), p. 222.

5. Edward Edinger, *Anatomy of the Psyche: Alchemical Symbolism in Psychotherapy* (La Salle, Illinois: Open Court, 1985), pp. 87-91.

Epilog to Part I

1. James Hillman, "Betrayal" in *Spring 1965* (Dallas: Spring Publications), pp. 57-76.

2. *Ibid.*, pp. 75-76.

Chapter Four

1. For severe depressions, physicians usually recommend treatment with a tricyclic antidepressant. This medicine, directed toward the central nervous system, is fairly safe and can improve sleep and appetite. Lithium carbonate, which alters the central nervous system's electroconductivity, has long been used to reduce the highs and lows of manic-depression. Phenothiazines are used in psychotic depressions to control agitation, insomnia and delusions. The controversial electro-convulsive shock therapy used to be the treatment of choice in severe depression. It is still used, but is combined with

new drugs to modify its side effects. A promising drug, Afranil, which cuts down the formation of obsessive thought loops in the brain, is being tested. Medication when necessary helps patients reach a state where the emotion no longer overwhelms their power to act and choose their own behavior.

2. Michael S. Gazzaniga, *Mind Matters: How the Mind and Brain Interact to Create Our Conscious Lives* (Boston: Houghton Mifflin, 1988), p. 122.

3. Marie-Louise von Franz, *Projection and Re-Collection in Jungian Psychology* (La Salle, Illinois: Open Court, 1985), pp. 9-11.

Chapter Five

1. Cf. Charles Tart, *Waking Up* (Boston: Shambhala, 1986).

Chapter Six

1. Edward Rice, *The Man in the Sycamore Tree* (New York: Double-day, 1970), p. 25.

2. Cf. M.F. Keyes, *Inward Journey: Art as Therapy* (La Salle, Illinois: Open Court Publishing Co., 1983).

3. Adapted from M.F. Keyes: "The Family Clay Sculpt in Redecision Therapy", *Transactional Analysis Journal*, Vol. 14, Number 1, January 1984.

4. Anthony de Mello, *A Way to God For Today* (Allen, Texas: Argus Communications video tape series).

5. *Ibid.*

6. C. West Churchman, *The Systems Approach and Its Enemies* (New York: Basic Books, 1979), p. 173.

7. De Mello, *op. cit.*

8. *Ibid.*

9. Anthony de Mello, S.J., *The Song of the Bird* (New York: Image Books, 1982), p. 1.

Chapter Seven

1. William Soskin, unpublished paper delivered at Vallombrosa Conference on Dante, November 14, 1976.

2. Cf. Helen M. Luke in *Dark Wood to White Rose* (Pecos, New Mexico: Dove Publications, 1975), p. 20. "It is not difficult to admit these...human weaknesses, to feel sympathy and pity, as Dante did, for those, including ourselves, who fall from desire into lust, from enjoyment of good things into greed, from spontaneous anger

into half-conscious cruelty. There is so thin a line between these things, and we do not want to know when we cross it; nevertheless, in admitting to our falls we are not yet in much danger of discouragement, and probably feel much relieved at having cleared away false guilt."

3. T.S. Eliot, "Burnt Norton" in *Four Quartets*, p. 15.

4. Joseph Conrad, *Lord Jim* (New York: Bantam Books, 1981), p. 138.

Chapter Eight

1. "143 countries engaged in 147 low-intensity wars during 1987." Tristam Coffin, "The Quest for Peace", *The Washington Spectator* (December 1, 1987), p. 1.

2. Michael Harrington, address at Network Legislative Seminar, June 1987.

3. Steven Kull, "Nuclear War and the Desire for World Destruction," *Political Psychology*, Volume 4, Number 3, September 1983, pp. 563-91.

4. Jane Wagner, *The Search for Signs of Intelligent Life in the Universe* (New York: Harper & Row, 1986), p. 18.

Appendix

1. Marie-Louise von Franz, *ibid.*, p. 177.

2. Donald T. Brown, "Teaching General Systems Theory in a Workshop Setting," *Living Groups: Group Psychotherapy and General System Theory*, James E. Durkin, ed. (New York: Brunner/Mazel, 1981), p. 284.

Bibliography and Suggested Further Reading

Agazarian, Yvonne M. and Richard Peters, *The Visible and Invisible Group*. Boston: Routledge Chapman & Hall, 1981.

Aligheri, Dante, *The Divine Comedy*, translated by John Ciardi. New York: New American Library, 1970.

Beck, Ariadne, "Developmental Process of the System-forming Process" in *Living Groups: Group Psychotherapy and General System Theory*, James E. Durkin, editor. New York: Brunner/Mazel, 1981.

Beesing, Maria, OP, Robert Nogosek, CSC, and Patrick O'Leary, S.J., *The Enneagram: A Journey of Self-Discovery*. Denville, NJ: Dimension Books, 1984.

Berger, John, *About Looking*. New York: Random House, 1980.

Berger, John, *Ways of Seeing*. London: Penguin Books, 1978.

Berger, Peter L., *The Homeless Mind: Modernization and Consciousness*. New York: Random House, 1974.

Berger, Peter L., *The Precarious Vision*. New York: Doubleday, 1961.

Berger, Peter L., *The Sacred Canopy*. New York: Doubleday, 1969.

Blank, Gottesegan and Gottesegan, eds., *Confrontation: Encounters in Self and Interpersonal Awareness*. New York: Macmillan, 1970.

Boorstin, Daniel J., *Democracy and its Discontents*. New York: Random House, 1975.

Bowlby, John, *The Making and Breaking of Affectional Bonds*. New York: Routledge Chapman & Hall, 1979.

Brown, Donald T., "Teaching General Systems Theory in a Workshop Setting" in *Living Groups: Group Psychotherapy and General System Theory*, James E. Durkin, editor. New York: Brunner/Mazel, 1981.

Northern California Group Psychotherapy Society, "Difficult Situations and Difficult Clients in Therapy Groups." University of San Francisco, January 16, 1988. Available through NCGPS, PO Box 227, Tiburon CA 94920.

Canetti, Elias, *Crowds and Power*. New York: Farrar, Straus & Giroux, 1973.

Capra, Fritjof, *The Turning Point: Science, Society and the Rising Culture*. New York: Simon & Schuster, 1982.

Catholic Bishops' National Conference, *Economic Justice For All: Pastoral Letter on Catholic Social Teaching and the U.S. Economy*. Washington, D.C.: Catholic Conference Inc., 1986.

Churchman, C. West, *The Systems Approach and Its Enemies*. New York: Basic Books, 1979.

Coffin, Tristam, "The Quest for Peace", *The Washington Spectator*, December 1, 1987.

De Mello, Anthony, S.J., *Song of the Bird*. New York: Doubleday, 1985.

De Mello, Anthony, S.J., *Wellsprings: A Book of Spiritual Exercises*. New York: Doubleday, 1986.

Diagnostic and Statistical Manual of Mental Disorders: DSM-III-R. Washington, D.C.: American Psychiatric Association, 1987.

Edinger, Edward F., *Anatomy of the Psyche: Alchemical Symbolism in Psychotherapy*. La Salle, Illinois: Open Court, 1985.

Eliot, T.S., *Four Quartets*. San Diego: Harcourt Brace Jovanovich, 1943.

Enright, John, "On the Playing Fields of Synanon," *Confrontations: Encounters in Self and Personal Awareness*, Blank, Gottesegan and Gottesegan, editors. New York: Macmillan, 1970.

Gardner, John W., *Self Renewal: The Individual and the Innovative Society*. New York: W. W. Norton, 1981.

Gazziniga, Michael S., *Mind Matters: How the Mind and Brain Interact to Create Our Conscious Lives*. Boston: Houghton Mifflin, 1988.

Goulding, Mary and Robert L., M.D. *Changing Lives Through Redecision Therapy*. New York: Grove Press, 1979.

Greene, Ford, *The Outline of Rev. Moon's Hand in Central America* (unpublished manuscript), 1988, available from HUB Law Offices, 711 Sir Francis Drake Blvd., San Anselmo, California 94960.

Guggenbuhl-Craig, Adolph, *Power in the Helping Professions*. New York: Spring Publications, 1971.

Hamaker, John D., *The Survival of Civilization*. Burlingame, California: Hamaker-Weaver Publications, 1982.

Haughton, Rosemary, *The Passionate God*. New York: Paulist Press, 1981.

Hersh, Seymour M., *The Price of Power*. New York: Simon & Schuster, 1983.

Hillman, James. "Betrayal," *Spring 1965*. Dallas: Spring Publications, 1965.

Hitchcock, John, *Atoms, Snowflakes and God*. San Francisco: Theosophical Publishing House, 1986.

Holland, Joe, and Peter Henriot, S.J., *Social Analysis: Linking Faith and Justice*. Maryknoll, New York: Orbis Books, 1983.

Holtz, Barry W., editor, *Back to the Sources: Reading the Classic Jewish Texts*. New York: Simon & Schuster, 1984.

Howes, Elizabeth Boyden, *Jesus' Answer to God*. San Francisco: Guild for Psychological Studies, 1984.

Johnson, Warren A., *Muddling Toward Frugality*. Boulder, Colorado: Shambhala, 1979.

Jung, Carl G., *Psychology and Alchemy*. Princeton, N.J.: Princeton University Press, 1968.

Jung, Carl G., *The Structure and Dynamics of the Psyche*. New York: Pantheon Books, 1960.

Kahn, Lynn S., *Peacemaking: A Systems Approach to Conflict Management*. Lanham, Maryland: University Press of America, 1988.

Keyes, Margaret Frings, *Inward Journey: Art as Therapy*. La Salle, Illinois: Open Court Publishing Co., 1983.

Kidron, Michael, and Ronald Segal, *The State of the World Atlas*. New York: Simon and Schuster, 1981.

Klerman, Gerald L. and Myrna Weissman, *Interpersonal Psychotherapy of Depression*. New York: Basic Books, 1984.

Kolbenschlag, Madonna, *Kiss Sleeping Beauty Goodbye*. New York: Bantam Books, 1981.

Kull, Steven, "Nuclear War and the Desire for World Destruction." *Political Psychology*, Volume 4, Number 3 (September 1983): 563-91.

Lewis, C.S., *Till We Have Faces*. San Diego: Harcourt Brace Jovanovich, 1956.

Lifton, Robert Jay, and Nicholas Humphrey, *In a Dark Time*. Cambridge, Massachusetts: Harvard University Press, 1984.

Lockhart, Richard, *Money and Soul*. Dallas: Spring Publications, 1983.

Luke, Helen M., *Dark Wood to White Rose*. Pecos, New Mexico: Dove Press, 1975.

Luke, Helen M., *Woman, Earth, Spirit*. New York: Crossroad, 1981.

Luke, Helen M., *The Way of Woman Ancient and Modern*. Three Rivers, Michigan: Apple Farms Publications, 1979.

Mahdi, Louise C., editor, *Betwixt and Between: Patterns of Masculine and Feminine Initiation*. La Salle, Illinois: Open Court Publishing Co., 1987.

Menninger, Karl, M.D., *Whatever Became of Sin?* New York: Bantam Books, 1988.

Millon, Theodore, *Disorders of Personality*. New York: John Wiley, 1981.

Naisbitt, John, *Megatrends: Ten Directions Transforming Our Lives*. New York: Warner Books, 1982.

Neumann, Erich, *Depth Psychology and a New Ethic*. New York: Harper & Row, 1973.

Olin, William F. *Escape From Utopia*. Santa Cruz, California: Peace Press, 1980.

Ouspensky, P.D., *In Search of the Miraculous*. San Diego: Harcourt Brace Jovanovich, 1949.

Palmer, Helen, *The Enneagram: Understanding Yourself and the People Around You*. New York: Harper and Row, 1988.

Parenti, Michael J., *Power and the Powerless*. New York: St. Martin's Press, 1977.

Peck, M. Scott, M.D., *People of the Lie*. New York: Simon & Schuster, 1984.

Phillips, Michael, *The Seven Laws of Money*. New York: Random House, 1974.

Rich, Adrienne, *On Lies, Secrets and Silence*. New York: W. W. Norton, 1979.

Rice, Edward, *The Man in the Sycamore Tree*. New York: Doubleday, 1970.

Roethke, Theodore, *Collected Poems*. New York: Doubleday, 1966.

Sabelli, Hector C., and Linnea Sabelli, *Process Theory and Psychodynamic Practice*. Chicago: Journal of Group Psychotherapy, Psychodrama and Sociometry MS.; Rush Presbyterian St. Luke's Medical Center, Chicago IL 60612, 1985.

Sanford, John A., *Evil: The Shadow Side of Reality*. New York: Crossroad, 1984.

Sanford, John A., *The Man Who Wrestled With God*. New York: Paulist Press, 1981.

Sayers, Dorothy L., *The Mind of the Maker*. New York: New American Library, 1956.

Schaef, Anne Wilson, *When Society Becomes an Addict*. New York: Harper & Row, 1987.

Sexton, Mary Patricia, CSJ, *The Dante Jung Correspondence*. Northridge, California: Joyce Motion Picture Co., 1975.

Solzhenitsyn, Aleksandr I., *A World Split Apart*. New York: Harper & Row, 1978.

Tart, Charles P., *Waking Up: Overcoming the Obstacles to Human Potential*. Boston: Shambhala, 1986.

Tart, Charles P., *Transpersonal Psychologies*. New York: Harper & Row, 1975.

Tuchman, Barbara, *The March of Folly*. New York: Alfred A. Knopf, 1984.

Von Franz, Marie-Louise, *Projection and Re-Collection in Jungian Psychology*. La Salle, Illinois: Open Court Publishing Co., 1985.

Wagner, Jane, *The Search for Signs of Intelligent Life in the Universe*. New York: Harper & Row, 1986.

Welch, John, O. *Spiritual Pilgrims: Carl Jung and Teresa of Avila*. New York: Paulist Press, 1982.

Journals and magazines

Dollars and Sense
International Journal of the Creative Arts in Psychotherapy
New Age
Spring
The Defense Monitor
Washington Spectator

Tapes

Carl Farber: *Liars and Lying* [Farber's address in Santa Monica]
Barbara Marx Hubbard: *Visions of the 21st Century* (New Dimensions Foundation).

Photo by Michelle Vignes

Margaret Frings Keyes is a psychotherapist in the San Francisco Bay Area. She has written extensively on crises in the life cycle and family legacy questions. Many of the exercises and techniques in *Emotions and the Enneagram* are adapted from her methods of therapy. Ms. Keyes is also the author of *Staying Married* and *Inward Journey: Art as Therapy.*

Book Order Form

Books by Margaret Frings Keyes

Send order to: Molysdatur / Publishers' Services
PO Box 2510 • Novato, California 94948

Please send the following order:

_____ copies of **EMOTIONS AND THE ENNEAGRAM:**
Working through Your Shadow Life Script.
ISBN # 1-882042-04-2 .... @ $12.95 each $ _____._____

_____ copies of **THE ENNEAGRAM CATS OF**
MUIR BEACH with illustrations by Fran Moyer.
An amusing set of intertwined allegorical stories,
this book embodies the Enneagram Personality
Classification System into the characters of nine
cats whose tales illustrate the foibles, defenses,
and virtues of each type. Purr-fectly funny!
ISBN # 1-882042-01-8 .... @ $9.95 each $ _____._____

_____ copies of **STAYING MARRIED**
This book provides practical techniques for
resolving conflicts and overcoming the defenses
which block deeper feelings in intimate relationships. Drawn from the fascinating experiences of
clients in her couples' therapy groups, the author
takes the point of view that most relationship
crises can be resolved. Crises are an important
element within marriage because the pain of crises
can be a source for new growth. We often back
away in pain and confusion when solution is just
within reach. What is at stake may be the needs of
only a portion of each partner's personality, not
the whole person, nor the relationship.
ISBN # 0-89087-902-8 .... @ $14.95 each $ _____._____

Ship to: (No PO boxes please)

Name _____

Address _____

City _____ State ___ Zip _____

Telephone (_____) _____
(in case we have questions about your order)

Payment: (check or money order)

Sub-total .... $ _____._____

Shipping .... $ _____._____
$2 first book; 75¢ each additional book

Tax (CA residents @ 7%) $ _____._____

Total Enclosed .... $ _____._____